Baby Stuff

Baby Stuff

a no-nonsense
shopping guide for
every parent's lifestyle

Ari Lipper and Joanna Lipper

Illustrations by Keun Shon
and Susan Canavan

Marlowe & Company
New York

Baby Stuff: A No-nonsense Shopping Guide for Every Parent's Lifestyle

Copyright © 2002 by Ari Lipper and Joanna Lipper

Published by
Marlowe & Company
An Imprint of Avalon Publishing Group, Incorporated
161 William Street., 16th Floor
New York, New York 10038

The baby products discussed in this book, and their model numbers, prices, and names, are current as of the date the book was written but are subject to change. The prices are meant to be a guide and may vary regionally. The author and publisher disclaim any responsibility for any of the products mentioned in the book.

Library of Congress Cataloging-in-Publication Data

Lipper, Ari.
    Baby Stuff: a no-nonsense shopping guide for every parent's lifestyle\by Ari Lipper, with Joanna Lipper.—Rev. and updated.
        p.cm.
    Originally published: New York: Dell Trade Paperback, ©1997.
    Includes index.
    ISBN 1-56924-527-4 (trade paper)
    1. Infants' supplies—Purchasing. 2. Consumer education.
    I. Lipper, Joanna. II. Title

RJ61.L599 2002   2002019666
649' .122'0296—dc21   CIP

10 9 8 7 6 5 4 3 2 1

Printed in the United States of America

Distributed by Publishers Group West

For Bari

Contents

Introduction   1

I. Getting Ready   7
Where to Shop   9
Product Safety Regulation   23
Borrowing for Baby   27
If You're Having a Nanny   31
Financial Planning   33

II. The Products   35
The Nursery   37
    Crib   38
    Crib Mattress   45
    Bassinet   47
    Cradle   51
    Changing Table   52
    Diaper Pail   57
    Rockers   60
    Baby Monitor   63

Layette   66
    Snapshirt   67
    Onesies   68
    Gown   69
    Stretchy   70
    Blanket Sleeper   70
    Cloth Diapers   71
    Hat   71
    Booties   72
    Receiving Blankets 72

Hooded Towels 73
Washcloths 74
Waterproof Sheet 74
Quilted Pads 75
Crib Sheets 76
Bumper 76
Crib Bib 78
Dust Ruffle 78
Comforter 79
Pacifiers 80
Pacifier Clip 81
Pacifier Case 81
Baby Manicure Set 82
Thermometer 82
Nasal Aspirator 84
Comb/Brush 84
First Aid Book 85
Bathtub 85
Bath Seat 89

Carriages and Strollers 93
Pram/Carriage 95
Carriage/Stroller 98
Umbrella Stroller 103
Jogging Stroller 106
Twin Carriage/Stroller 108

Getting Around 114
Infant/Toddler Car Seat 117
Infant Car Seat 121
Car Seat/Stroller Travel Systems 125
Front Carrier 128
Sling Carrier 132
Backpack 133
Infant Seats 138
Swing 141
Walkers 144
Jumpers 147
Portable Crib 149
Diaper Bag 154

Food 159

  Nursing Pillow 160

  Nursing Stool 161

  Breast Pump 163

  Nursing Pads 167

  Breast Shields 168

  Bottles and Nipples 168

  High Chair 173

  Booster Seat 178

  Mealtime Accessories 181

Safety 185

  Outlet Plugs 186

  Corner Guards 187

  Safety Gates 188

  Drawer, Cabinet, and Toilet Locks 190

  Door and Stove Knob Covers 192

  VCR Lock 192

  Cord Holders and Shorteners 193

III. Appendices 195

  When Will You Need It? 196

  Different Products for Different Budgets 198

  Manufacturers and Catalogs 202

Index 207

Introduction

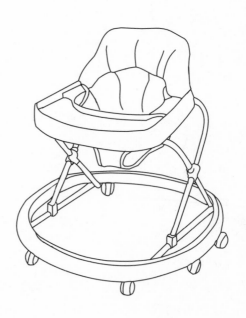

If you're reading this book right now, you're probably very close to one of the most significant and dramatic life changes you'll ever encounter. With the pregnancy and the labor, the questions you'll have about raising your child, and all that's involved in actually doing it, becoming a parent is loaded with anxiety. The last thing you need to worry about is all that you have to buy for the baby.

But every day I saw people like you in my store, wide-eyed, more than a little confused, and definitely overwhelmed by the strange products and brand names. Friends and relatives had been giving them advice on every aspect of having a baby, which always included what to buy. "You should get this," and "You have to have that," and "This is the only kind to get" floated through their minds as they tried to decide how to spend thousands of dollars on things they knew very little about. My job was to help them get a little perspective and to work with them so that, without ending up in the poor house or the nut house, new parents got the equipment they really did need to keep their babies healthy and happy for their first year of life.

Reading this book should give you a good understanding of the products that are out there, how they work, which ones are necessities, and which ones are best for you to consider based on your lifestyle. The Preparation chapter covers where to shop, product safety, the ins and outs of borrowing baby products, and product-related things to keep in mind if you're hiring a nanny. I also touch on financial planning for your new bundle because, believe it or not, college is just around the corner! The biggest section of the book covers baby products, broken into the six main areas: the Nursery, the Layette, Carriages and Strollers, Getting Around, Food, and Safety. I rate each product as either a Must Have, a Might Want or a Totally Optional. Must Haves are things that you, well, must have. There are choices you'll have to make about which brand or style or price range you want to buy in, but, for example, you must have a crib. On the other hand, you might want a rocker. You and your baby will both live if you don't have one, but many people opt to get one—that's how I'd define a Might Want. The Totally Optionals are the frills, the specialized products like jogging strollers and wipe warmers that are not really important, but some people like them. I also let you know up-front the price range for each item, when you'll need it, and whether or not it's something that's good to borrow. You'll notice that some items have a broad price range, starting at the very low prices available at the big chain stores. The tips I provide here are the same tips I shared with my own customers that saved them hundreds, if not thousands, of dollars and kept them coming back to my store.

During my eight years of selling baby products at a baby store in New York City, I tried to give my customers a sense of their power as consumers. There's a tremendous variety of products and immense competition in this industry between retailers and manufacturers. Retailers should be very interested in working with you and in providing you with excellent service, or they don't deserve your business. Manufacturers have 800-numbers and customer-service operators who are "standing by" to answer your questions. I've included a Resource Guide that lists the phone numbers and websites of the major manufacturers of baby products as well as the regulatory agencies that oversee them. Make full use of these numbers and whatever services the companies offer; they can be of invaluable assistance to you in purchasing decisions and proper product use.

You don't need to read this book from cover to cover. It is intended to be a reference tool that you can open again and again as you shop. Keep in mind that the prices quoted are approximate and are only meant to give you a frame of reference. To help you plan your buying, there's an Appendix with different layettes for three different budgets—a top-of-the-line, a middle-of-the-road and a penny-pincher. This should let you take a big-picture view and help you decide where you want to spend more and where you want to cut corners.

I always advised all parents not to shop too early. Some people run out to the store as soon as they see that little stick turn blue, but ten months (not nine, as you've learned by now) is a long time. Wait to get over the shock first, then start shopping. On the other hand, this isn't something to simply get out of the way. As overwhelming as all this shopping can be, it should be fun and exciting. Don't rush through it. Generally, you can get everything you'll need within eight weeks of placing an order, but I recommend visiting a store about twelve weeks before your due date. There are also many things that you don't have to make a decision on until after you've had the baby, and even months down the road. The second Appendix is a graph that will show you the usual time period that you'll need each of the major products in the book. Taking time into account should let you concentrate on what you need and when you need it, allowing you to stagger purchases so you can let your credit card take a breath.

I must admit I used to run in the other direction when a customer walked into my store with his or her nose in a book or consumer magazine. Usually these people wouldn't take any of my advice because they had already made up their minds. This book should not be the last word on anything for you, although there are a few things that I'm pretty adamant about, as you'll soon see. What I want to do is educate you about this vast baby product industry so that when you are ready to shop you won't be feeling overwhelmed and flying blind. This book will get you to think about your lifestyle and needs, which will help you clarify the types of items that you should consider, but it won't take the place of a good store with experienced, helpful salespeople. Their knowledge and expertise shouldn't be discounted; instead, I hope this book prods you to ask them questions and build a relationship with them.

You might be wondering if I have any children of my own. My wife and I have a 22-month-old daughter named Bari; however my knowledge comes from experiences that occurred long before she arrived. I spent eight years servicing a multitude of nervous new parents, receiving feedback day after day about what worked for people and what didn't, which products were reliable, practical, and useful. I have seen how virtually every baby product works over time in real life—not just in one family but in thousands. I interject some opinions that come from my own usage of certain products, however the information you'll be reading doesn't come from just one couple's experience or lab tests done by men in white smocks; it comes from thousands of people just like you.

I hope the information in this book is as useful to you as it has been to my customers, and I wish you luck on your journey into parenthood.

—ARI LIPPER

Getting Ready

BEFORE YOU EVEN begin thinking about what to buy and when, you should begin to consider where you might shop. Additionally, this chapter covers some basics about product safety, borrowing and things to keep in mind if you'll have a nanny. Lastly, I've included a brief discussion of financial planning because you actually might begin saving for college before Junior's first birthday.

Where to Shop

FACE IT. YOU'RE going to spend a lot of money on this whole baby deal. I'll try to help you save money in this book, but even if you're on the low end, even if you can borrow nearly everything you'll need and breastfeed your baby until he's playing Little League, you'll still be spending hundreds of dollars on baby products. If you're on the high end, you'll be in for many thousands of dollars. That's before the braces, before the college fund, before kindergarten. Most of you fall somewhere in between, which means thousands of dollars spent in the eighteen months between finding out that you're pregnant and baby's first birthday.

Consumers have many options regarding where to purchase baby equipment. In this discussion, I'll go through the pros and cons of buying from independent stores, chains, and catalogs, discuss best buys from each, and help you understand the power you wield as a consumer.

Independent Stores/Small Chains

A good independent juvenile products store is a key element of your buying strategy. Let's think again about just how much money you're spending here and what you're spending it on. You're paying out anywhere from five or six hundred dollars up to thousands, and it's for your baby. If you were buying a stereo or a computer or even a used car for that much money, you'd be asking about more than just the products; you'd want to know about the store you were buying it from as well. You're going to want to know about repairs, reliability, the helpfulness and courtesy of the staff, delivery, and return policies. You'll want to feel comfortable about asking questions, and in the beginning, you'll probably be asking the staff of your baby store as many questions as you'll be asking your pediatrician.

The service at almost any independent store will beat the chains on all of those counts. A reputable local retailer can educate you about products, consult with you about your lifestyle and needs, and guide you through the important buying decisions. You should also be aware that buying baby products is not a one-time event. No one pulls the van up to the doors of the Baby Superstore and drives away with everything they'll ever need, all working perfectly. A new parent's reality is that you'll buy some things, but you won't know what other people will get you, so you'll have to go back regularly to buy what you really need. You'll change your mind a few times; the baby will hate a couple of products; one or two might not work. You won't understand how to open or shut or latch or assemble any number of things you'll buy. Some will come in bad colors. You'll be torn between the cute one and the one that makes more sense. You'll lose an important part to something. Can you picture the teenage assistant manager at a big chain store showing you for the seventh time how to collapse your baby's carriage? In other words, the relationship that you develop with a store will need to last long after your initial $2,000 order, and a store should be interested in keeping your business. For your day-to-day needs, I recommend establishing a relationship with an independent or small chain baby products store close to your home.

Of course, not all stores are alike, so let me run through some services and features that you should keep in mind as you're making your selection. If the store you're considering doesn't offer these services, I suggest that you keep looking.

What To Ask

When you begin your store selection process, there are many things to ask. You interview pediatricians, so why not baby stores? I recommend that you do an initial screening over the phone. The following is a list of things to find out before you even bother visiting a store:

❏ **Do they take credit cards?**
❏ **Do they allow you to pay a balance with a credit card over the phone?** (For example, if custom or space constraints don't allow you to keep any baby furniture in the house until after the baby is born, you might leave a $500 deposit on a $3,000 order. The last thing a new daddy is going to feel like doing after twenty-eight hours of labor is run to the store to give his credit card for the balance.)
❏ **How much of a deposit do you have to leave?**
❏ **Is your deposit refundable** if you change your mind about purchasing some or all of what you've ordered?
❏ **Is the store flexible** if you want to change your order, for example, from white to natural furniture?
❏ **Do they take phone orders with a credit card?** This is especially convenient after the baby is born when you will need endless odds and ends.
❏ **Is there a delivery charge,** and what is the minimum for delivery? It might be snowing, you might be alone, and you might need a pack of nipples.
❏ **How long will it take the store to deliver** once your baby is born? The correct answer is delivery within two days.
❏ **Does the store's delivery people also assemble furniture?** Is there a charge for this?
❏ **What is the return policy?** Will they credit your card or will you only get a store credit?
❏ **What are the store hours?** Are they convenient for you? The store may be open 9 to 5, but if you work 9 to 5, that just leaves you with the weekends to get anything you need, and sometimes you'll need things immediately.
❏ **Does the store stock products you already have in mind,** brand names you have heard of, styles that you like?

What To Look For

Once you have screened a few stores, go and visit. Go prepared, gather some comparative prices for items from catalogs, ads, magazines, and friends to see how the store stacks up. Though independent stores do tend to be more expensive than chains, there's no reason that they should be way out of line with other independent stores in your area. If you think you're being ripped off every time you walk in the door, you should probably walk out and find a better store.

There are other things for you to check for or ask about:

❏ **See if there is a large selection of items on the floor.** In some stores, there are few floor models—you select merchandise out of catalogs. I don't recommend a store that has a limited amount of merchandise on the premises for you try out. As you'll see later in the book, some important items you'll be buying must be fitted to your size, needs, and preferences. You won't be doing anyone a favor if you return half of what you ordered because you don't like it. Remember, they pay people to make things look good in catalogs. You would never buy a car without test-driving it first.

❏ **Find out if the store has a complete layette department** so you won't have to go to a lot of different places to get all your shopping done. Check the Layette section of the Products chapter for a complete list of what that entails.

❏ **An on-premises repair department** is a very important feature in a store. You don't want your stroller to be sent away for weeks to another state while you're left holding little Edgar.

❏ **Speak to the salespeople to see if they are helpful, courteous, and interested.** You're going to be asking these people a lot of questions, some of which may seem painfully stupid, even to you. If you're not comfortable with the salespeople, you'll either feel like a fool half the time—and why should you?—or else you may not ask the questions that turn out to be essential.

❏ **Don't be oversold.** Does the person waiting on you seem only to recommend the highest-priced items in each category? Does the line "Of course, you want what is best for your baby" keep creeping into the conversation? Once you've read this book, you will know that many of the highest-priced items are not the best for you or your baby, and this salesperson might not be the best for you, either.

Special Services

To me, a store's stock, policies, and ambiance earn a customer's trust and repeat business, but special services can really distinguish it from other product stores. Some are simply conveniences; others can prove to be true life savers. You can do fine in a store that doesn't do some of these things, but you might wish that it did.

❏ **Can you register for gifts?** This prevents duplication, and you may even get what you would buy. If not, it makes returning gifts less painful. A fair number of retailers offer this, and it's a very popular service, both with new parents and with those giving gifts. Mom and Dad get what they need, and the gang at work doesn't have to guess what would be the best baby gift to get them.

❏ **If you are pressed for space, some stores will hold gifts for you that you don't need right away,** like a high chair that you won't need for the first five months.

❏ **Another convenience is being able to set up a house account** so that your nanny or caregiver can purchase things without your needing to be there and without having to hand over your credit card.

❏ **In the lifesaver department, the store should provide customers with loaner items** when their order hasn't arrived, or when they need to use an item once and really don't want to buy it. For example, since many of my urban customers didn't own a car but needed a car seat just to take the baby home from the hospital, I would lend the car seat. I've had customers who were

> ▶ **TIP:** The best product is not always the most expensive one or the least expensive one. The best product is the one that works best for you and your baby.

going away for the weekend and needed an extra portacrib or stroller, so I've loaned them floor models. This is the type of service that I would expect from a store where I am a loyal customer, and you should expect it as well. Of course, you should only expect accommodations like these if you really are a loyal customer. Buying a two-pack of nipples every few months will not establish you as a familiar face. Also, don't expect a $1,200 English pram when your $70 umbrella stroller is sent off for repair. Let's be honest, the store owner is doing you a favor.

❏ **Location** is the final important factor in selecting a baby store. The closer the store is to your home, the better off you'll be. If you have any kind of problem with your furniture, you'll be much more likely to get quick service. If you shop very far away, you might have to wait until the next time the repair person is in your area and who knows when that will be? Distance is, of course, relative. If you live in a city, the difference may be between a store three blocks away and one on the other side of town, but if you're in the suburbs, it could be three miles versus ten. And it never seems wise to drive three hours to save $20.

What To Buy At An Independent Store

You should purchase the items that you use the most and that may require servicing at your neighborhood retail store rather than at the big chains. Use this store to purchase items that you need a fairly extensive education on, such as a stroller, which can be complicated to fold, or items with many features to understand.

I went on an undercover spy mission to a chain store to check out the strollers. I discovered a new meaning to chain store—all the **strollers** were chained to the shelves. Sure, it stops thieves from rolling out with the top-selling model, but it also prevents shoppers from an aisle test-drive to see which stroller would be most comfortable. Then, when a salesperson asked if I needed any help, I asked her how to fold the stroller. She tried her best but couldn't fold it. The stroller is not a good item to purchase without experienced sales help, so a local store is your best bet. Of all the items you'll buy, the stroller is the most likely to need frequent servicing. Before you buy a stroller, you should make sure that the store has an on-site repair department or can provide you with a loaner in the event that yours must be sent out for servicing.

> ▶ **TIP:** If your baby store does not service strollers, you can call any stroller manufacturer to get the name of a local store that can provide you with repair services.

Nursery furniture is another good item to get from your local retailer. Even though you are not likely to need frequent repairs on furniture, you may need the ball bearings on your glider rocker tightened or the tracks adjusted on your dresser or changing table drawers. You'll also benefit from the information that the staff can give you, such as how to master one-hand operation of the crib. The store will deliver and assemble the furniture for you, too. They can also help when it's time to disassemble and properly store the furniture for your second child, often for the price of a tip. For the same price, they will usually help you with the reassembling as well when the next child comes along. You might be missing some parts by then, and you can get replacements, often free of charge, if you've been seen around the store often enough.

A **glider rocker** is worth buying from a local retailer. Over time, the screws can loosen. If your chair does not glide the way it did originally, the store can help you.

A **front carrier** is an item that you should try on before buying. Often people don't wear them properly, so they are uncomfortable and, therefore, don't get used for very long. It is helpful to have a knowledgeable salesperson to assist you. Also, in a small store they will probably let you walk around with your baby in the carrier for a half hour to make sure you really like it. You may not be able to do that at a chain store. The same goes for a baby backpack. However, this doesn't prevent you from checking out chain store prices once you've decided on a carrier that you like.

If you are nursing, a **breast pump** is a good item to buy or rent from your local store. There's probably a knowledgeable person on staff who has heard the same questions you will ask from hundreds of mothers. Your breast pump may need servicing, and the store most likely keeps parts in stock. When you're nursing, you can't afford to be without a pump.

Once you know which bottles and nipples baby prefers, you might do better buying at a chain. However, you can get some valuable assistance with **bottles and nipples** at your local store. The salesperson can introduce you to your various options and share feedback from other parents. When you initially investigate this product category, it would be helpful to start at your local store.

The best reason to buy from an independent store has nothing to do with any particular item. There are certain things that are worth buying at big chains because the chains get volume discounts that a small retailer could never compete with. But if you spend $2,000 in Toys "R" Us, you can't go up to the gum-chewing clerk at the cash register and ask what kind of a deal you can get. With a small retailer you still have some bargaining power, especially if you're placing a large order. You don't need to turn the store into a Cairo bazaar, haggling over the price of feeding spoons, but there's often some play. Try for ten percent and hope the owner tosses in a black-and-white toy.

The Big Chains

Having just made fun of adolescent salespeople at the big chains, I will make up for it by admitting that lots of their prices are hard to beat and you should definitely stock up on certain staples and even make some big purchases there. I recommend buying items that do not require an education or the help of a knowledgeable salesperson. These items include a swing, playpens like the Pack 'N

▶ **THINGS YOU SHOULD DEFINITELY TRY OUT BEFORE BUYING:**

You should not buy certain items sight unseen from a manufacturer's catalog in a store. If these products are not on display for you to see, touch, and "kick the tires," you should go to a place where you can see them first—even if you go back to the first store to place the order (if the price, service, or stock selection is better.) These items include the stroller, especially since you might need some education and practice in the folding process; the rocking chair, which had better be comfortable for those 2 a.m. feedings; the crib; and other nursery furniture.

Play, Exersaucer, walker, bouncer, bathtub, bathseat, diaper pail (or Diaper Genie), safety products, certain layette items, bottles, nipples and pacifiers (once you know your brand), nursing pillow, and baby monitor. It's a good idea to look at the circulars in the Sunday newspapers; you may spot a needed item that you were thinking of getting anyway on sale at a big chain. For example, it seems that three times a year Toys "R" Us has a sale on the Sport Pack 'N Play for around $80. That's one-third less than full retail price. The Exersaucer, a very popular item, has been seen periodically for $49 at Toys "R" Us, considerably less expensive than the independent retailers price. But beware when you buy an Exersaucer at a big chain: it may be the same one that your neighbor's kid didn't like. To be safe, make sure the box of any potential purchase isn't obviously retaped. If it looks retaped it's possible that when you lug it home it might be missing a part. Big chains would generally make you trek back to them or refer you to the manufacturer.

And if you think you'll have trouble with a missing part for an Exersaucer, try calling a big chain with a stroller problem. If you decide to buy your stroller from a big chain, be prepared to deal with the stroller manufacturer yourself and possibly travel or ship it very far away to have it repaired without the courtesy of a loaner. This could prove to be a dreadful inconvenience.

I wouldn't buy any big, heavy items at large chains because, to keep costs down, the stores don't always deliver or can't deliver right away.

However, I want to emphasize the potential savings that can be found at big chain stores. As I mentioned before, any item that does not require experienced sales help could be substantially discounted at a chain. You can even take advantage of the product knowledge of an experienced salesperson at an independent store, and then check the prices at the chains.

Juvenile Products Superstores

Juvenile products superstores are similar to other big chains in some respects. They offer very competitive prices, the sales personnel are often not very knowledge-able, and you may find items that have been returned and re-boxed awaiting another purchaser. However, unlike the big chains that have a juvenile products depart-ment (like Consumer's Distributing, Toys "R" Us, Service Merchandise), superstores are giant 50,000-square-foot facilities fully dedicated to merchandise for babies. You can get virtually everything you would ever need in the bright, well-laid-out aisles of a baby superstore: nursery furniture and decorations, strollers, car seats, monitors,

---

THE FIVE COMMANDMENTS OF BABY SHOPPING

1) Don't buy anything in a rush. There's always time.

2) Don't let anyone else hurry you into buying anything. You want to do business with people who let you make deci-sions, not people who try to force you into them.

And for those with impatient grandparents, I add:

2a) Even if they're paying.

3) Try whatever you need to try. What have they got to hide? Are they too busy to help you? If they won't let you check out the merchandise, go someplace where they will.

4) Allow the salesperson to believe that you are only the tip of the iceberg. You have friends/sisters/cousins who are all pregnant and you will send them all to this person if you like the service. Also, hint that you have several residences to fill with baby furniture—this might give you some bargaining power.

5) Don't destroy any of the original packaging. Something may not be to your liking after you open it. You may get the same thing from a friend three days later that you won't be able to return without a receipt, but you'll have a receipt from your original packaging.

bathing equipment, feeding equipment, clothing, toys, formula, lotions, wipes, detergent, diapers—you name it. These stores usually offer a wide selection of major brands, a gift registry, and other services.

When you are looking at prices in superstores, you might find that they seem fairly reasonable for some items, but keep in mind that there are hidden charges (such as delivery and assembly) that could even the playing field between a superstore and an independent retailer or small chain. For example, you might find that the crib that you are considering is $50 cheaper at Babies "R" Us, but delivery costs $50 and there might be yet another charge for assembly. They might also make you pay in full up-front, whereas another type of store might require only a deposit. Again, you have to weigh the pros and cons of all shopping venues, and you will probably end up buying from several different types of stores.

Catalogs/Online Shopping

The best thing about this type of shopping is that you don't have to go anywhere. You can sit there in your jammies, sipping cocoa and ordering up a storm from all the great-looking stuff. The problem is, as I've pointed out, there are items such as strollers that you need to examine and try out before you buy. If you stay away from those purchases, you can often do fine shopping by catalogs or online. Since inventory requirements aren't as stringent as for retailers, catalogs often have feature products that stores might not have. It's easier for catalog merchandisers to take a chance on an unusual item. For example, the Right Start catalog sells a cover that keeps a car seat cool while the car is in the sun. This is a pretty useful thing to have around, but generally a retailer won't stock this kind of specialty item until enough people ask for it. Catalogs are also good if you need out-of-season merchandise. For example, if you are taking a beach vacation in the winter, you may not find sand toys or flotation aids in stores with only seasonal stock, but catalogs would have them. Another benefit of catalogs is that you can return purchases under just about any circumstance.

There are many catalogs and websites targeted at the juvenile market, and new ones come out all the time. The main categories are usually clothing, toys, and safety items, or a little of everything. Popular baby and children's clothing catalogs include Hannah Anderson (www. hannahanderson.com, 800/222–0544); Lands' End Kids (www.landsend.com, 800/356–4444), which also offers other merchandise like a very popular diaper bag; and L. L. Bean Kids (www.llbean.com, 800/341–4341).

Of the many toy catalogs, some standouts are Lillian Vernon Kids (www.lillianvernon.com, 800/285–5555), which features some nice personalized toys and other gift items. Back to Basics (800/356–5360)which is heavy on wooden toys and lots of things you thought they stopped making once you grew up, like Nok Hockey and springy horses. There are lots of online options for toy shopping and two of the easiest to navigate are the recently-resurrected E-Toys (www.etoys.com) and Amazon.com (www.amazon.com). Both of these sites are segmented by the child's age and give a wide selection of product categories such as learning, building, musical, ride-on, visual, electronic, etc.

For safety items, the two most popular catalogs are Safety Zone (safetyzone.com, 800/999–3030) and Perfectly Safe (perfectsafe.com, 800/837–KIDS). These are good for new parents to browse through to get ideas and to start thinking about what they will need to do to baby-proof their homes. Before buying, however, I would ask my knowledgeable baby store salesperson and my pediatrician about the necessity of some of these items.

The two most popular general catalogs are Right Start

(www.rightstart.com, 800/348–6386) and One Step Ahead (www.onestepahead.com, 800/274–8440). You might want to call to obtain copies of some of these catalogs, not to buy immediately but to get an idea of what's out there. You might see something that you hadn't thought of or that you want to get more information on.

It won't be long before you are on every juvenile catalog's mailing list and email list, and, if you actually buy anything, you'll probably be on twice.

Garage Sales

You might be one of those people who like to go to garage sales on the weekends. I'm a big advocate of borrowing from friends and loved ones, but I really can't see the value in buying a stranger's castoffs for your baby. Generally, garage sales are not to make money but to get rid of junk. This is not a smart strategy for accumulating baby products. Are you going to set out in the morning looking for a used car seat? Borrow all you want from friends who can tell you something about what you'll be using, but I wouldn't recommend buying any used equipment at garage sales for your baby (except maybe a charming antique music box), just to save a buck.

▶ **MOST POPULAR BABY GIFTS:**

Chances are someone will give you: a front carrier, monitor, bouncer seat, Pack 'N Play, Boppy, activity gym, black-and-white mirror, black-and-white toys, clothing, gift certificate.

Time Frame For Ordering

You have plenty of time before ordering furniture to pick a store that you are comfortable with. It should not take more than eight weeks to get any item you order, and most purchases should take only four weeks, so you don't have to buy in the first store you go to.

Product Safety Regulation

NEVER LEAVE YOUR CHILD UNATTENDED!
I'll repeat that one more time, in case you missed it.
NEVER LEAVE YOUR CHILD UNATTENDED!

There is no substitute for your attention. This is the most important thing you should know about your baby's safety.

Even with that precaution, safety must still be your first priority in selecting baby products. In the Products section I describe safety requirements for each item, so you can be sure that you're buying something safe for your child to use.

But where do these requirements come from?

You might be confused and even anxious about product safety regulation and how it affects the purchasing decisions you will make. While I will get down to more safety specifics when I review the products, this section provides you with an overview of the safety regulatory bodies and organizations and important safety issues. This way, when you're shopping and you come across safety seals and other such documentation, you'll be better able to decipher what they really mean and make purchases that will work best for you.

The CPSC

The U.S. Consumer Products Safety Commission (CPSC) is an independent federal regulatory agency established by the Consumer Product Safety Act enacted in 1972 to safeguard the public against unreasonable risks of injury from the use of consumer products. In addition to protecting the public, the CPSC assists consumers in evaluating the comparative safety of consumer products, develops uniform safety standards for consumer products, and promotes research into the causes and prevention of product-related injuries. With the exception of child safety seats, juvenile products are under the jurisdiction of the CPSC.

To protect the public, the CPSC:

- Requires manufacturers to report defects in products that could create substantial hazards
- Requires, where appropriate, corrective action with respect to specific substantially hazardous consumer products already in commerce
- Collects information on consumer product–related injuries and maintains a comprehensive Injury Information Clearinghouse
- Conducts research on consumer product hazards
- Encourages and assists in the development of voluntary standards related to the safety of consumer products
- Establishes, where appropriate, mandatory consumer product standards
- Bans, where appropriate, hazardous consumer products
- Conducts consumer outreach programs for consumers, industry and local governments.

Product safety has come a long way. At one time, federal law prevented consumers from suing manufacturers of defective products because the items were not purchased directly from manufacturers but from a third party, namely retailers. This law has been changed and now manufacturers are responsible if their products cause injury. Consumers do not have to prove manufacturer negligence, just that they suffered an injury. This change has caused manufacturers to place a much greater emphasis on safety. A large part of the CPSC's regulation centers on voluntary requirements imposed by the manufacturers themselves.

The JPMA

The Juvenile Products Manufacturers Association (JPMA) is a nonprofit lobbying organization that serves as a self-policing body for the industry. The JPMA offers certification programs for high chairs, play yards, carriage/strollers, walkers, gates/enclosures, portable hook-on chairs and full-size cribs. JPMA certification serves as extra assurance to consumers, by the presence of a certification seal and listing in a directory, that products are in compliance with standard consumer safety specifications. The standards for these product categories were written by American Society for Testing Materials International (ASTM International), a nonprofit organization. Industry members work with the CPSC and consumer groups to develop the standards.

Obtaining and maintaining JPMA certification is a costly and time-consuming pain in the neck (and lower areas), and therefore many products don't have it. This doesn't mean that they don't comply with ASTM standards—it is mandatory for all products in these categories to meet ASTM requirements. Many of the products I recommend are not JPMA–certified and yet they function perfectly well without any safety problems. If you call the JPMA, they will tell you that just because they do not certify a product does not in any way imply that it is not safe—product safety is federally regulated and JPMA certification is totally voluntary.

Car Seats

The safety of car seats is of particular concern to new parents. The **National Highway Traffic Safety**

Administration (NHTSA), under the U.S. Department of Transportation, was established to carry out a congressional mandate to reduce the number of deaths and injuries resulting from motor vehicle crashes. The NHTSA sets the federal safety standard for car seats, and their safety performance has been validated many times over in real-world crashes. There are individual state car seat laws as well that pertain to the age requirements for car seat use. Most safety problems with car seats result from improper installation. I will go into detail about proper installation in the Products chapter on car seats.

When purchasing a car seat, you can feel confident about its safety, as long as it is labeled "This child restraint system conforms to all applicable federal motor vehicle safety standards" and the stamp of manufacturing is dated after January 1, 1981. If you borrow a car seat, make sure it too has the proper labeling and date of manufacture. You should always call the manufacturer to find out whether the product has been recalled and to obtain a current instruction manual. If it has been recalled or if it doesn't have the mandatory label—**don't borrow it!**

Recalls

When you buy a baby product, there is no way of knowing whether it will be recalled someday. Although product recalls are very rare, it's always a good idea to mail back your product registration card. That way, in the unlikely event of a recall, you'll be notified directly by the manufacturer. Recalls are often due to some modification that a product needs to make it safer. This is another good reason to register with the manufacturer—they might send you a part to install yourself. Product recalls are usually publicized heavily in the media, and all retailers that sell the product are required to post a recall notice and remove the product from their shelves.

Use A Little Knowledge
And A Lot Of Common Sense

Many of the safety guidelines outlined by the Consumer Products Safety Commission and other organizations are based on the premise that no product is safe if you leave your baby unattended. All the regulatory organizations have 800-numbers and hotlines and fax-on-demand literature services, and they all stress this basic yet crucial idea.

That should sound like common sense to you—if not, here's your wake-up call. It should also give you a little perspective on the frenzy that surrounds baby product safety right now. If you'd never consider leaving your baby alone in the tub or letting him play on the stairs or helping you fry chicken, then you're probably going to take all the reasonable precautions as they arise.

As I said before, the CPSC regulates the safety of consumer products, and there are many safeguards and requirements in place to assure that the products you purchase are safe, but don't substitute these regulations for your own intuition and examination of the products you will use for your baby. I wholeheartedly recommend borrowing, but you should absolutely take the simple precaution of calling the manufacturer (see the Resource Guide for phone numbers) to make sure that the item has not been recalled and that it complies with all safety requirements.

Borrowing for Baby

A COUPLE OF WELL-DRESSED, well-groomed women were in the store one day looking at carriages. One was pregnant, the other had a two-year-old, and both appeared as though they could have bought anything—if not everything—in the place. They asked for help, so I began showing them different models, and each time I wheeled out another, the mother-to-be's friend gushed about how much she had loved her Emmalunga Viking when little Jennifer was a baby. The Viking is a nice carriage: traditional, with large wheels, a removable bassinet and convertible stroller piece. It retails for $300, and since it has the bassinet feature it's really worth $400. I had to agree with her that it was a good product.

With all the heavy lobbying from her experienced friend, it didn't take long to see that the Viking was going to win out. My customer-to-be was ready to sign up, when I looked at her friend and said, "Why don't you lend her yours? You're not using it anymore."

Clearly neither of these women had ever been told not to buy something. They both stared at me for a few seconds as though I were completely insane, especially the friend. Apparently the thought of borrowing or lending had never crossed their minds. If you're having your first baby, your first reaction might be the same. You're having a brand-new baby and you want everything to be as perfect and new as she'll be.

And then one day the Visa bill will come.

Your child will stay perfect, but suddenly some compromises will be in order. For many, borrowing is a necessity, and for everyone else it simply makes good sense. Borrowing baby equipment and clothing is the ultimate costcutter for parents. If you borrow good things, you won't have to compromise in giving your baby the highest quality creature comforts.

Borrowing some strategic items will also keep you from trying to buy everything at once. I've seen a lot of people nearly melt their credit cards when they furnish an entire room of their home and store up everything their child will need for the first year all in one day. I recommend accumulating your nursery items over time, the same way you'd decorate any other room in your house. You can see how your taste develops as you live with the things you already have, and then see what you and your baby need to make the nursery complete. It should be reassuring because, as a parent-to-be, you're in a vulnerable position. Borrowing some things acts as a check on your desire to buy everything you see in the catalogs you'll start getting in the mail every day. Also, there's something daunting about picking out all these dozens of objects, making sure they match, timing their delivery with your delivery, and on and on. Borrowing can help ease your mind, buy you some time, save you some money, and, trust me, your baby will never know the difference.

The best items to borrow are expensive and durable, yet **have a short span of usefulness.** At the top of the list are the **large carriage/stroller.** Better models cost over $200, and most people use them for less than six months before switching to more convenient umbrella strollers. Another good item to borrow is the **infant car seat.** You must have some sort of car seat to bring your baby home from the hospital. This isn't a particularly expensive item, but your baby outgrows it in about six months or at 20 pounds. The **front carrier** falls in here, too, since babies outgrow them fairly quickly, also at about 20 pounds. Though they're made of fabric, they're worn high and tend not to get as dirty as other fabric items. Borrowing items like a carrier can be part of your learning experience—you get to comfortably test a product to see if it suits your baby and deserves your money. The same goes with the **backpack.** If you borrow a carriage, infant car seat, and front or back carrier, you'll save somewhere between $300 to $400.

Whenever possible, I suggest borrowing the carriage and car seat before the baby is born. This will give you time to figure out how they work and determine whether or not they need to be refurbished before your baby can use them. Refurbishing is a relatively simple matter. If you need to find the manufacturer, check the Resource Guide; I list phone numbers with brands and models. Place your phone order for replacement parts, such as wheels, liners, or boot for a carriage, or a clean cushion for the car seat, and you'll only have to waddle as far as your front door to get them. Before borrowing a car seat, contact the manufacturer and confirm that they are still making that model. If not, it may not meet current safety standards, a fact that they will tell you.

A crib and a changing table are also great things to borrow, if a little harder to come by. If the furniture has been dismantled and stored, be sure that you have all the parts to reassemble them, and the instructions. Finding missing pieces isn't hard: many stores will have extra parts for models in production, or you can ask the manufacturer to ship a whole set of hardware and instructions. That may be surprising, but more than most industries, the makers of baby products seem to take a longterm view and assume that a lot of their bigger items end up being passed along. And if you're happy with the service on your used Graco product, you'll be more likely to buy a new Graco product in your next toss-up. If the manufacturer doesn't make that model anymore, ask why they've stopped making it, so you can be assured that it meets all current safety guidelines.

As you'll see further along in the book, I also recommend borrowing the **high chair, bouncy seat, swing, bassinet,** and **rocking chair.**

Clothes are a very tempting and popular item to lend and borrow, but they are tricky. It is virtually impossible to return baby clothes in the same condition you got them. Between the baby's normal wear and tear and countless cycles in the washer and dryer, in most cases you'll be lucky to hand back something that's a bit stretched out of shape and faded. I've heard of people who put their name

on the tags before lending clothes and I would not recommend borrowing from them. Ideally, they should
simply give you the clothes. Or else you'll be too nervous
to ever put your kids in them or, God forbid, your baby
spits up on some T-shirt, and you find yourself at the Gap
buying new clothes for the lender while your kid is still
wearing the used outfit. Tragedies don't always happen,
and borrowing clothes doesn't have to be a problem, but
the bottom line is that the gift of used clothes is better
than the favor of lending them.

For hygienic reasons, you should buy **bottles, nipples,
pacifiers,** the **bathtub** and **newborn toys** such as rattles,
small stuffed animals, and anything else that will spend
time in baby's mouth. These are all fairly inexpensive and
usually last only long enough for one child's use. The same
goes for **safety products** such as outlet plugs and the like.
You'll never forgive yourself if something goes wrong just
because you wanted to save $1.69. I also don't recommend
borrowing **mattresses.** Again, they're not that expensive,
and they tend to be the last line of defense in the toilet-
training process, so they get mildewy and saggy. Save a few
bucks on something else and go new here.

My final advice on borrowing: Don't be afraid to ask.
There are few times in your life when you'll need so
much help and people know that. Take advantage. The
baby store will still be open and you'll still probably
spend more there than you have to.

If You're Having a Nanny

IT'S NORMAL NOW for both parents to work. That means
that many of you will be paying someone to watch your
baby while you're at the office. You'll be home before and
after work, and on the weekends, which is a healthy
amount of time, but you're still sharing the responsibilities.

So it makes sense for you to include the nanny or babysitter in your buying decisions. In return for this consideration, you should expect them to develop the same level of competency and responsibility in using these products as you have.

Usually a nanny does not begin work until the mother returns to her job, so there will be many purchases in the first two months that will not involve the nanny. If you already know who will be providing child care for you, though, you should bring them along. I've heard it said that planning the wedding is a necessary test for engaged couples to see how they'll handle problems, and the same could be said here. An afternoon of stroller shopping may tell you a good deal about how you and your nanny will interact on everything from keeping schedules to what little Trudy will wear today. Chances are that the consideration you'll be showing by inviting her opinion will go a long way toward establishing an honest and open working relationship.

You should absolutely get your nanny's approval on some tools of the trade. To me, the umbrella stroller is an important item for the nanny to be comfortable with because she'll be using it the most. Umbrella strollers are a few months down the line, so you should be able to bring her along. Other items worth getting the nanny's input on are the high chair and feeding utensils. She'll be feeding the baby at least one meal per day, so why shouldn't she use something that works best for her?

Whether you've included your nanny in these decisions or not, it is vital that you are confident in her ability to operate everything that you've bought. Take the time to show her how to fold the stroller, work the crib, secure the car seat, whatever. These are the tools of her job and she should know how to use them, but it is as much your responsibility to ensure that knowledge as it is hers to have it.

You should also make clear any preferences and rules about certain items. This is important when it comes to the things that help pacify the baby, such as swings and walkers. These are not meant for extended use, but the sad fact is that some babysitters do just that, just as some parents do.

As I mentioned earlier, it might be convenient for you to set up an account at your local store that the nanny can use. It beats spending hours in the store, especially on the weekends when it's the most crowded. If she turns out to be a compulsive shopper, you can always return things.

Baby Nurses

There are pros and cons regarding baby nurses, all of which I'll steer clear of right now, but one issue concerns me: a lot of people tell me that the nurse often provides them with a supply list filled with items that don't seem necessary. Who knows? Your nurse might have just come from a stint at a Rockefeller's home where they had every item known to man. Consult your pediatrician and your store to see if the list seems realistic, and purchase what seems essential. You can always fill in later. A better solution is to request her list before your due date, just to get an idea of what she thinks you should have on hand when the baby comes home.

Financial Planning

WHILE YOU'RE THINKING about which stroller to buy and whether or not to register for a wipe warmer, you might begin to consider arranging a meeting with your financial advisor. According to the U.S. Department of Education, the cost of a college degree for today's newborn could exceed $200,000 for a private university and $80,000 for a public university. Therefore, college savings should begin as early as possible to maximize the future return. There are various approaches to college savings and your financial advisor will present these to you. Since financial planning is definitely not the focus of this book, I will not address any details here but I just wanted to describe one area that is very new and considered exciting by people who are excited by these things. Even if you aren't one of these people, it's still worth looking into.

The newest college savings vehicle, authorized under Section 529 of the Federal Internal Revenue Code, is called the 529 Plan. A law enacted in June of 2001 frees most 529-plan withdrawals from federal income taxes, starting in 2002, if the money is spent on qualified higher-education costs. Under the old law, your account's earnings were taxed at your child's tax bracket when they were withdrawn for college costs. Granted, a child's tax bracket is usually the lowest one, around 10%, however in 18 years the extra 10% can be a considerable sum that can be put toward the education expense.

Unlike many other programs, there are no income limits with a 529 Plan—all investors can participate regardless of their income or net worth. Additionally, the account is in your name—not the child. The child is named as the beneficiary. In fact, another family member such as a grandparent can open an account and name the grandchild as the beneficiary. The beneficiary can change at any time without any penalties so if your child decides to travel the country on a bus with his rock and roll band instead of going to college, you can use the money for another child's education.

There are 529 Plans in most states and they should be in every state by the end of 2002. You are not required to join your own state's plan, however you might get a state tax deduction—it depends on the state. You can compare the different plans and decide which one is best for you. Again, you should sit down with a financial planner sooner rather than later to start this process.

The Products

The Nursery   37

Layette   66

Carriages and Strollers   93

Getting Around   114

Food   159

Safety   185

The Nursery

ASSEMBLING THE BABY'S nursery is a big task, not just because of how much you have to get, but also because of all the considerations involved. You're decorating a room in your home and you want it to look just right, but at the same time it has to work for the little person who'll be gnawing on much of it within the year. And then there's your budget, whatever it is. Given that you could use a Louis XIV secretary for a changing table, there's no limit on what you can spend here. A lot of the big-ticket items you'll be buying are in this section—namely, the crib and the changing table—so smart shopping here isn't just helpful—it's necessary if you plan to buy anything else for your kid.

A few things to remember when you're shopping for these items:

❏ You're buying furniture and household appliances, so even though they may have clowns painted on them or play music, use the same care and common sense you use to choose products for other rooms.

❏ While some of these things seem fairly specialized, remember that there are often more common (read: cheaper) items that serve just as well. I'll offer some practical substitutes throughout.

❏ Unlike most furniture you buy, nursery items outlive their primary usefulness quickly. You may spend an absurd amount of money on a dining room table, but you can say with some certainty that if you so choose, your grandchildren will be eating off of it in 35 years or so.Little Marvin, though, will not be filling out his Harvard application on the changing table. It may sound sensible to spend $600 on a piece of living room furniture, but maybe it's not a wise investment for an item that you'll only use for two or three years. If you can't borrow some of these things or substitute, at least try to consider whether you can recycle the item from its nursery role so it "grows up" with your child.

Crib

> • Must Have
> • Birth to 2 years, or when child can climb out
> • Good to borrow
> • Price range: $200 to $600
>
> ## Essentials
> ▶ a drop side easily operated by one hand
> ▶ adjustable mattress height

A CRIB IS a crib. No matter if you pay $200 or $600, it's going to do the same thing, which is to keep your baby safely in one place while you lie in your bed and wish he were asleep. The crib is the most important piece of furniture for your nursery, and one of the easiest to buy. You do have choices in styles, some functions, and whether or not the crib can be converted to a bed later, but since all new American cribs are built to meet the same safety guidelines, you don't need to bring your measuring tape to the baby store. Do it if it makes you feel better; after measuring five or six, you'll see that every crib is basically 55 inches long and 30 inches wide, and every mattress is designed to fit these cribs. The exception to this rule is IKEA's models or European cribs not made to U.S. specifications. If you buy one of these cribs, you'll have trouble finding a mattress and sheets and bumpers in the U.S. that will fit, and Sweden's a long way to go for bedding.

Take with a grain of salt those publications that rate certain models of cribs from one manufacturer higher than other models made by the company. Actually, every crib from a given manufacturer is made the same way, and your decision should boil down to style and budget. Consider it a piece of furniture you will be living with for a couple of years and buy what you like to look at.

Safety First

American-made models must meet certain standards. You should get some peace of mind from ASTM F1169, the Standard Consumer Safety Specifications for cribs:

❏ **Never use a crib with corner posts higher than $\frac{1}{16}$ of an inch above the end panel.** Babies can strangle if their clothes get caught on posts. If the posts on your crib are higher than they should be, unscrew them or saw them off, and the remaining end panel should be sanded smooth. This doesn't apply to corner posts over 16 inches above the end panel, such as canopy posts.

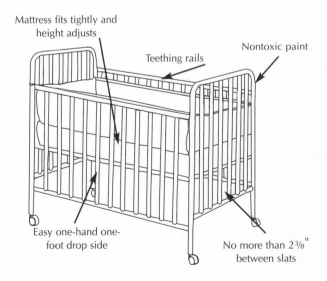

Mattress fits tightly and height adjusts

Teething rails

Nontoxic paint

Easy one-hand one-foot drop side

No more than $2\frac{3}{8}$" between slats

❏ **Crib slats or spindles should be spaced no more than 2⅜ inches apart and none should be loose or missing.** You don't want the baby's hand, foot, or head to get wedged in and stuck. The simplest test of the width is that a soda can should not fit between the slats.

❏ **The mattress should fit snugly, with no more than two fingers' width between the edge of the mattress and the crib side.**

❏ **Always keep the drop side up when the baby is in the crib.**

❏ **Never place your crib near draperies, blinds or wall-mounted accessories with long cords,** because a baby could become entangled in them.

I have a few more Must Haves of my own:

❏ **A drop side easily operated by one hand.** This way, your other hand is free to scoop the baby in and out. With domestic models, you might have to use your foot to move a kick bar to release the drop side. Be sure you're comfortable with how the drop side works; you'll use it a lot. Every model made by a given brand will function the same way, so you just need to decide which brand's mechanism you prefer, and then choose the style you want.

❏ **Adjustable mattress height,** so it lowers as the baby grows taller. That keeps baby in babyjail as long as possible without his being able to climb out and wake you up at 3 a.m. for some Cheerios and a viewing of *Toy Story.* The mattress should lower to as many different positions as possible. High-end American cribs such as Simmons and Child Craft have four positions, while Italian and Canadian-made cribs have only two. Check that there's a significant difference between the highest and the lowest settings, because the lower the mattress sits, the longer Junior will be secure in the crib.

You Might Want It To Have

❏ **Wheels** let you move the crib around while you wrestle with the bedding. Since the mattress fits so snugly in the frame, it's not as easy to change the sheets as you may think; you'll want all the elbow room you can get. Don't make the mistake of thinking that once your crib is assembled you'll be able to wheel it from room to room around the house. A crib is wider than the doorway, so be sure to decide which room the baby will sleep in before the crib is delivered.

❏ **Teething rails** are another practical feature of domestic cribs. The imported models don't have them, supposedly for aesthetic reasons. The paint used on cribs is nontoxic, but you probably still don't want your child eating much painted wood. A teething rail will help the crib from looking like it was set upon by a family of beavers.

If You're Borrowing

❏ Be sure any crib you borrow is new enough to meet current safety guidelines.

❏ Check carefully for any rusted metal hardware. There's a lot of metal under the springs that you wouldn't think you'd have to worry about, but it can get jostled loose.

❏ All screws should fit tightly. The drop side and kick bar should work only in conjunction with one another. In other words, you should only be able to lower the side if you release these two things at once.

❏ If you're assembling the crib, be sure you have all the hardware and instructions, or else contact the manufacturer for replacements. If you're borrowing an imported crib, find yourself an Allen wrench—one of those L-shaped metal tools, four or five inches long, with four sides—or be certain it's included. Don't ask me why, but the Italians and Canadians don't make cribs with regular screws.

❑ If you need help in assembling the crib, don't hesitate to ask. Dad may have dreams of being Bob Vila or Norm Abrams, but this is not the place to test his actual furniture-making abilities. You should feel free to contact your local baby furniture store and ask for some help.

❑ If someone else assembles the crib, pay very close attention. You will probably be the one who will do this the next time if you ever move or have another baby.

Should You Get A Crib That Converts To A Bed?

The idea sounds good, but I don't recommend buying a certain crib model just because it converts to a bed. After all, you have no way to know what you and your child may want two or three years after you buy the crib. You may move, redecorate, or, most important, have another baby, in which case Baby Number One will have to give up his bed to Baby Number Two. It could be five or six years before you ever get to use the convertible feature, at which point you may very well want to look at something other than the same gnawed-up crib.

And why pay big bucks for a convertible crib when a new generation of toddler beds that take crib mattresses retail for as little as $50.

Another touted feature of convertible cribs is the built-in drawers on the side or on the bottom. In reality, these drawers are not made with the kind of skill as the drawers in your cabinets. They're usually just wood on wood, without runners, and they're in an inconvenient place. They tend to warp, and now that manufacturers have stopped including dust covers on them everything gets yucky under there. If you ignore everything I'm warning you about and go for the drawers, just store only those things that you don't need daily, such as extra sheets. I still think you'd be better off storing things in a closed box that gets shoved under the dust ruffle and spring of a regular crib.

As this convertible decision basically runs along foreign or domestic lines, there are a few more things to keep in mind.

> ▶ **TIP:** If your crib is delivered with a malfunction, report it immediately. Otherwise, if you wait five months, the retailer will assume it's your fault and will rarely replace it at that point. If there's a problem that can be fixed by **replacing** a certain part, let the retailer replace just that part—don't insist on a whole new crib. Keep in mind that cribs are not assembled in individual components like a car. Every part from the same style crib is interchangeable. If you make it easier on the retailer here, he or she will be that much more willing to help you out when you need a favor down the line. And you will need favors.

❏ Cribs basically come in either white or natural wood. I recommend natural wood. It doesn't chip like white furniture, it ages better, and if you space your kids out and have to store the crib, the more basic look will keep it from going out of style. The problem with Italian cribs here is that they don't match with domestic pieces, no matter what the finish. If you decide to have a white nursery and you buy an Italian-made crib, know that it is a very high gloss white and may not match other white elements in the room. The same goes for the foreign natural wood cribs; if you choose to mix and match one with some less expensive pieces, you'll mix, but it won't always match.

❑ If you decide to buy an Italian crib, make sure it operates easily with one hand. The drop sides of older Italian cribs have two little pulls, one on each side, which can be harder to operate than the standard domestic styles.

Your Budget

There are a number of other functional considerations that account for the wide range of crib prices, though convertibility is the main factor. One is the number of drop sides the crib has; two cost more than one. For most people this is a not an issue, because they push cribs against the wall. The theory is that two drop sides will make it easier to change the sheets, and while I think you'll welcome any help you can get here, the fact is that you'll still have to lift up the mattress, making the two drop sides kind of moot.

Another reason for the price differences is the weight of the wood used in particular cribs, but don't confuse weight and cost with quality or usefulness. If you choose a less expensive crib made of lighter wood, it won't necessarily be flimsy or fall apart. On the other hand, some Italian cribs weigh a ton, cost an arm and a leg, and are merely laminated particle board. If the lighter wood is the only thing keeping you from a cheaper crib, go ahead and save money here, rather than paying extra for something that may not even be solid wood.

The final major reason for cost differential is style. The practical side of me thinks this is crazy, since your kid couldn't care less about Italian styling or the sturdy look of natural wood. But since this is a piece of furniture you have to live with, it's not unreasonable. Just hope that your tastes aren't quite the same as the manufacturers; the cribs they deem most "stylish" or most "designed" do go for more than the more basic models.

In the top price ranges are cribs in wrought iron that can run over $1,000; Italian imports that are convertible with drawers underneath and high-gloss finishes. An example of a high-priced import would be the Bonavita Pamela at $530. In the midrange there are many choices by Sorelle, such as the Leonardo ($399) or the Mission by Simmons ($430), a nice mission style crib. All of these feature one handed drop sides, an important feature.

The budget-conscious have many good choices. Three good products, all at $249, are the Lisa and the Sherry, both from Bonavita, and the Simmons Matino. The Bonavita cribs both feature a drawer and are convertible to a bed. All three feature one handed operation as well.

Crib Mattress

- Must Have
- Birth to 2 or 3 years
- Not good to borrow
- Price range: $80 to $149

Essentials
▶ square corners
▶ waterproof covering
▶ ventilation holes

THE MATTRESS PURCHASE is fairly simple because you only have two choices—foam or innerspring. You should consult your pediatrician on this, but the basic wisdom gives the top pick to a hypoallergenic, firm mattress. The firmer, the better, because it won't "give" and let a baby sleeping on his stomach sink into the mattress and block his breathing. Your doctor, like the American Academy of Pediatrics, probably recommends that you prevent your baby from sleeping on her stomach because it increases the risk of

Sudden Infant Death Syndrome (SIDS). Additionally, with a firm mattress the baby is less likely to get his hands and feet caught between the edge of the mattress and the crib (see "The Crib" for guidelines on the space allowed between the crib frame and mattress). You don't have to worry about the hypoallergenic part, since all new mattresses manufactured today are hypoallergenic.

Because it is very difficult to change the sheets on crib mattresses, I recommend foam; it's lighter and therefore easier for the person changing the sheets. Most parents I tell this to seem surprised when I recommend foam, mostly because their backs begin to ache just thinking about sleeping on it. Try not to project your personal mattress needs onto the baby mattress purchase, though. For all those awful orthopedic reasons better kept between you and your chiropractor, your baby doesn't need as good a mattress as you do.

It Must Have

If you're buying a foam mattress, it must have:

❑ **Square corners** so there are no gaps to trap baby's limbs
❑ **A waterproof covering**
❑ **Ventilation holes** to prevent cracking.

Your Budget

If you still want an innerspring mattress, they are generally priced from $50 to $150, and usually come with very long warranties. Foam mattresses range in price from $50 to $100.

Accessories

There are products available that keep a baby on his side while sleeping. They consist of two soft, wedge-shaped

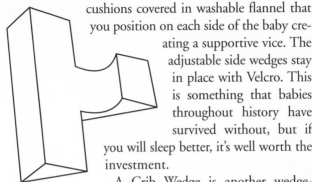

Crib Wedge

cushions covered in washable flannel that you position on each side of the baby creating a supportive vice. The adjustable side wedges stay in place with Velcro. This is something that babies throughout history have survived without, but if you will sleep better, it's well worth the investment.

A Crib Wedge is another wedge-shaped piece of foam that goes beneath the crib sheet under the baby's head to raise the head if he is congested. This is the only acceptable method for raising the baby's head, because a pillow is a suffocation hazard.

Bassinet

- Might Want
- Birth to 3 months
- Good to borrow
- Price range: $40 to $100

Essentials
▶ snug-fitting mattress

IF YOU INTEND to use a bassinet, you won't have to run around like a crazy person to make sure that you have a crib as soon as you get home from the hospital. Essentially just a basket around two and a half feet long, a foot and a half wide, and a foot deep, a bassinet has firm sides, a hard bottom, and a thin mattress inside. Some have handles and some are mounted on wheeled frames.

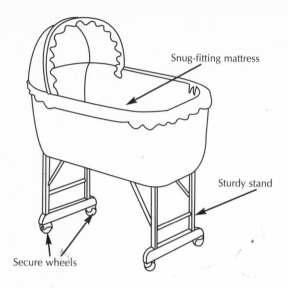

Snug-fitting mattress

Sturdy stand

Secure wheels

The main reason to use a bassinet is convenience. During the first few months, you won't want to be too far from your baby. Of course, given how many times she'll need to be fed and changed, being too far from your baby won't be something you'll have to worry about, but on the off chance that you get a stretch of two or three hours' sleep, you'll probably want that bassinet nearby, especially if you're breast-feeding. Many people believe that a newborn feels more secure in a bassinet for the first few weeks. This may sound like an old wives' tale, but it may make sense: If you were just pulled out of such a cozy, warm spot, the last place you'd feel comfortable in would be the wide expanses of some massive, white crib. The bassinet will be a snug, secure place for the baby to sleep while she's still getting accustomed to this whole life on earth business. If you are not using a bassinet, you can buy crib wedges (wedge-shaped foam inserts anchored with Velcro that act as a supportive frame) to keep the baby centered in the crib. Bassinets are great to borrow because they are used for such a short time.

Safety First

❏ Just like a crib, it is important for a bassinet to have a **snug-fitting mattress** so that the baby cannot become wedged between the mattress and the side of the bassinet.

You Might Want It To Have

❏ A nice feature on some bassinets is a **removable Moses basket** that separates from the base. Poetically named after the basket that Moses floated down the Nile in (did you see the movie?), this is useful for carrying the baby around the house if there are stairs or to take him to a friend's or relative's house if you are all going for dinner.

❏ It is useful to have a **storage shelf** under the bassinet.

If You're Borrowing

Since a new mattress costs about $20, I would suggest making the investment if the bassinet has been in storage for a while or has gone through many babies. Before ordering a new mattress for a bassinet, make a paper template of the basket interior and bring it to the store. This will ensure a perfect fit. Make sure that the bassinet's stand is sturdy and that, if it is on wheels, all four are firmly attached.

Your Budget

Since the bassinet is an item that is only used for the baby's first few months and doesn't get a lot of wear and tear, it's a great item to borrow. You should also keep your eyes open for special deals; department stores often offer a bassinet free or at a greatly reduced price if you buy a certain amount in their baby department. It makes sense, as long as you don't buy more than you originally planned and you're not paying a lot more than you might in a discount store.

I recommend a regular Badger bassinet #776 ($50 to $75). This is the simplest and least expensive. Crafted from woven wicker, the basket comes complete with vinyl liner, mattress, and folding legs for easy storage between babies. It also has a removable hood. This basically describes every bassinet, regardless of price. The difference between this one and one that costs, say, $100, is the size of the overall basket, and the unit's wheels, additional features such as a removable Moses basket or a storage shelf, and whether or not linens are included. The Kidsline Bebe Fina ($129 to $149) model offers a removable Moses basket with a foldable stand. These are available in a wide variety of fabrics.

Don't worry about the mattress. Just one or two inches thick, it seems so thin; but a newborn won't even dent it and he certainly won't suffer orthopedic problems in the first eight weeks. The basic bassinet mattress measurements are 14 inches by 31 inches and bedding is available specifically for bassinets. Make up a bassinet the same way as a crib, with a waterproof sheet and a quilted pad (you should have two of each; $5.99 each), a cotton sheet (you should have three or four; $4.99 each), and a bumper ($15 to $25). In lieu of a bumper, you can also purchase a bassinet liner that has a half-skirt for around $30. As you can probably guess, I don't recommend that you decorate the bassinet with the kind of floor-length eyelet skirt that retails for $60 or even more. That's $60 you could be spending on something either more fun or more useful.

Cradle

- **Might Want**
- **Birth to 4 months**
- **Good to borrow**
- **Price range: $129 to $500**

Essentials
▶ same safety specification as cribs [see p. 39]
▶ snug-fitting mattress

A CRADLE IS slightly different from a bassinet. A cradle is slightly larger (the mattress dimensions are 18 inches by 36 inches) and it is not always on wheels. Basically, it's a wooden basket suspended on a frame. The main advantages of a cradle are that it is bigger, so you will be able to use it for a month longer than a bassinet, and it can be rocked gently to soothe an agitated baby. (Keep it stationary by inserting the included peg). A possible disadvantange is that, as some believe, if your child learns to fall asleep by rocking, you'll be rocking her to sleep until her husband takes over. Aesthetically, you are offered white or natural wood, as well as metal and brass. This can be helpful if you are interested in matching the cradle to a nursery decor. The main disadvantage is that it must be made up in the same manner as a crib. You must use a bumper, while most bassinets are lined and don't need one. Proper size sheets and pads are available.

Safety First

❑ **A cradle must comply with the same standards as a crib** (see p. 39) with respect to the distance between any slats. There must not be a space of more than 2⅜ inches.
❑ **The mattress must fit snugly** to prevent the baby from becoming wedged between the mattress and the side of the cradle.

If You're Borrowing

This is a great item to borrow; however, a lot of cradles have been in someone's attic for a very long time. You may want a new mattress and you should measure the distance between the slats, as the one you're borrowing might be some kind of an antique and not up to safety code. Make sure: all the hardware is there, including the pin or peg, so that it can be stationary if desired; none of the hardware is rusty; and the cradle sits securely on its frame.

Your Budget

Just like the bassinet, a cheaper cradle is better. The most budget-conscious choice is to borrow, but if you don't have any friends or relatives with a cradle collecting dust in their garage, then the least expensive choice if you are purchasing one is the Standard Cradle by Sorelle ($99). Sorelle also makes the Dondola Gliding Cradle featuring a gliding motion ($189). On the high end are specialty cradles in brass and other ornate metals. And as with like in cribs, the price difference is strictly based on style, not function.

Changing Table

- Might Want
- Birth to toilet trained
- Good to borrow
- Price range: table—$89 to $500   pad—$15 to $30

Essentials
▶ comfortable height
▶ broad, flat surface

ANYTHING CAN BE a changing table—a countertop, kitchen table, or bed, even the floor of the ladies' room at your favorite restaurant. Your nursery will definitely need a flat, stable, wide surface high enough for comfort on which you can change young Roscoe's diaper, but what you do not necessarily need is a piece of furniture called a "changing table." You can buy, or you may already have, a piece of furniture like a low dresser or table, for example. To make this a changing table, you can use a three-inch-thick indented foam pad on top of it. This pad is encased in quilted vinyl, has a strap to keep the baby in place and snaps onto the back of a dresser. An example is the Rumble Tuff changing pad that retails for $25 to $35. There are also add-on kits that convert any piece of furniture to a flip-up changing table which can be removed after it is no longer needed ($129 to $179). Since there are so many alternatives to conventional changing tables, don't buy a changing table just because you've seen it pictured with your crib (life is not a furniture catalog). If you're going to

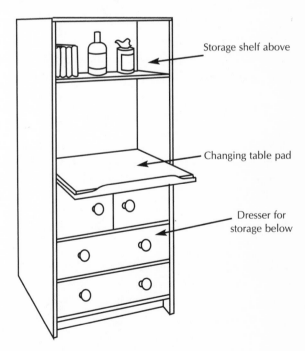

Storage shelf above

Changing table pad

Dresser for storage below

purchase a piece of furniture devoted to this purpose, you should first be sure that you like it as a piece of furniture. The changing table will still be a piece of furniture long after the crib is gone and the baby is out of diapers, so it makes sense to buy something that you can use later.

It Must Have

❑ The most important thing about a changing table is **height.** You will be spending a lot of time in front of this table, so it should be at a comfortable height, approximately belly button–level.

❑ **A broad, flat surface will give you enough room to work on** and a better chance of catching a baby in danger of rolling off. You're going to be diapering Rodney until he's toilet trained, so you'll need a big enough area to handle a squirmy, resistant toddler.

❑ **If the changing table and dresser are separate pieces, make sure they are securely fastened.** You might have read that a changing table must have a raised lip on the end or a strap to keep the baby on the table. Remember Chapter Three! Never leave your child unattended. You will never leave your baby on the changing table while you go and answer the door, even if the baby is strapped down like Frankenstein. You will always be holding the baby on the table. Always. Plus, the lip in front is very annoying. You'll bang your elbows and baby will bang her head.

You Might Want It To Have

❑ I recommend natural wood as opposed to white. White chips and it tends to crack when it gets wet (and chances are very good that this item will be getting wet).

❑ If you are purchasing a changing table with drawers

underneath, try to find drawers with metal glides to ensure an easy slide, and locking mechanisms so that the drawers don't come flying out when you pull on them.

❑ Though it seems like a good idea, steer clear of hutch pieces above the changing surface. Yes, you can store things in it, but an active baby stands a very good chance of hitting his head on it at some point. If you want your powders and lotions in front of you, install a small shelf above the changing table.

Your Budget

As I said, anything can become a changing table, and if budget is a big concern try transforming a piece of furniture you already own or can justify buying and still using after diapers are a distant memory. However, if you would like to get something designed specifically for this purpose, you can purchase the Badger Deluxe Foldaway for $99. Available in natural wicker or white, this is similar to changing tables used when we were babies—the changing area folds out and there are several storage compartments underneath that flip out. When closed, this unit takes up very little room. Imported changing tables on wheels with one drawer and two shelves underneath range in price from $129 to $199. Some come with as many as three drawers and one shelf.

Morigeau and Ragazzi are two French-Canadian companies that make higher-end changing tables that convert to high-quality, attractive three-drawer dressers ($450 to $550). If you like the look of the dresser (as many people do) and feel that it will be useful after your child graduates from diapers, then the Morigeau or Ragazzi would be good choices. But keep in mind that you are spending about $500. You might want to spend that money on a piece of furniture that you like better and use it with an indented pad, or you might want to wait to spend that money until your child has an opinion on decorating her room. Parents often came into my store with a preschooler eager to toss out the "baby stuff."

Additionally, keep in mind that if you plan to spend that kind of money on the changing table/dresser, you will probably end up purchasing all the complementary pieces from the same manufacturer (not that there's anything wrong with that, I just want you to understand all your options). That usually means a chest of drawers and an armoire, which includes a hanging bar and two adjustable shelves. These two pieces will generally set you back around $1,000. I recommend that people wait a while to order these. They are not a necessity when you come home with the baby and only take six to eight weeks to deliver.

Changing Table Accessories

Five extras that some people love. If they make sense to you, try them.

Laundry Bag—There are special laundry bags that drape over the side of the changing table and are fastened with Velcro. These are washable, and retail for around $6.99.

Lucite Organizer—This item also hangs off the edge of the changing table for storing lotions, wipes, and powders ($12.99).

Terry Covers—You should cover the plastic changing mat with a layer of material to prevent the baby from sticking to the mat and also to absorb any moisture that results from changing the baby. You know what I mean. A terry cloth cover serves this purpose, but I don't feel it's worth $20, since it's really just a terry cloth with an elastic hem so it fits the pad perfectly.

Using a towel and tucking the ends under the changing pad would serve the same purpose.

Chucks ($8.99 for pack of 25)—Chucks are disposable, plastic-filled paper liners that you place directly under baby's tushy when changing a diaper. This way you won't have to change the terry cover every time.

Lap pads ($4.99 for two)—These are flannel-encased rubber pads, 12 inches by 14 inches, designed to do the same thing as chucks, but are obviously less expensive and more environmentally friendly. The bad news: you have to wash them.

Diaper Pail

- Must Have
- Birth to toilet trained
- Not good to borrow
- Price range: $16 to $30

<u>Essentials</u>
▶ Foot pedal
▶ A locking mechanism
▶ A filter or deodorizer

WHAT CAN I SAY? You take the bad with the good, and this part of parenting certainly falls into the bad. What you'll most want here is something that's easy to empty so you'll do it often enough that the diapers won't begin to smell, and something that won't smell if you're too repelled to do it as often as you should.

With one exception, diaper pails aren't all that different, but there is one big decision you have to make, and that's whether you should use disposable or cloth diapers—convenience and dryness versus the environment. Other, greater minds have addressed this topic, so I bow out of the debate, but if you use a diaper service for cloth diapers, you will be sent along a metal cylinder into which you put the soiled diapers. The service empties it every week. Without getting too graphic, you must flush as much waste as possible out of a cloth diaper in the toilet before depositing it into this metal cylinder. If you decide on cloth, you'll figure this out quickly. If you go disposable, you've got several choices.

It Must Have

You will be extremely sorry if your diaper pail does not have:

- **A foot pedal** for easy opening
- **A locking mechanism** of some kind to keep the dog or an older child from using the dirty diapers as a soccer ball

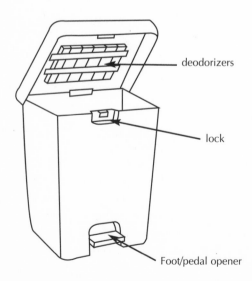

❑ **A charcoal filter** or **nontoxic deodorizer cake** for odor control. Charcoal filters are a pain to change and last about three months, but they are the best for controlling the odor (yes, there is an odor).

Your Budget

It is possible to save money here if you really want to. Just use a regular garbage pail and control the odor with nontoxic deodorizer cakes. Go to a hardware store and get a covered Rubbermaid-type garbage can. It comes in lots of colors, so you should have an easy time matching your nursery.

Otherwise, on the low end of the ready-made diaper pails, there's the Safety 1st Odorless diaper pail ($15 to $20). This is a simple push button pail. A product that I would not recommend in this category is the Diaper Champ by Baby Trend ($29.99). My wife and I renamed this item the Diaper Chump. It's huge, and extremely difficult to open, which is good so that the baby can't get to it, but you get tired of the painful indentations in your fingers every time you open it. I lasted about two months before retiring this item to the incinerator room.

On the high end, there's the latest rage in diaper disposal—the Diaper Genie ($25) (Major Nelson not included). While three rubs on the pail won't get that doody diaper to disappear, the Diaper Genie is able to hermetically seal each soiled diaper in scented plastic. You open the lid and stick the diaper into a small cylinder, then you twist the lid and the diaper is forced down into the barrel of the Genie. When it is full, you end up with something that looks like a chain of fat, white sausages. Although this pail is the best at odor control, it requires more of a "hands-on" process with the diaper than traditional disposal methods, something which you might find distasteful. If you have an environmentalist friend visiting, I advise you to hide the Diaper Genie, because this contributes even more nonbiodegradable plastic to the landfill. The fact that the Diaper Genie retails for $10 more than other diaper pails is not enough to bump it to "high end" status: It's the price of the disposable bag refills, $4 to $6 for 30 to 60 toddler-size diaper changes, that makes this an expensive undertaking.

Accessories

An item that could be considered part of the diaper pail family is a **hamper** for your nursery. These are generally small, ugly wicker numbers that almost reach your knee and don't hold much of anything—not even tiny baby clothes. The wicker type retails for $25 to $30, but you may be better off getting a Rubbermaid laundry basket (to match your Rubbermaid diaper pail).

Rockers

- Might Want
- Birth to redecorating
- Good to borrow
- Price range: $99 to $499

A ROCKING CHAIR is a cozy addition to the nursery. You'll need a chair in there, so it might as well be big and comfortable and relaxing. The question is when you should use it. As you probably know by now, everyone has an opinion about baby issues, and, believe it or not, that extends to rocking your baby. Some say you should rock the baby to sleep, but others say that then the baby will need to be rocked to sleep every night and, more to the point, at 3 a.m. when he wakes up crying. Then again,

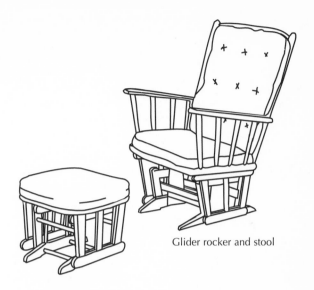

Glider rocker and stool

I've heard that rockers are particularly good for babies with colic. Ask your pediatrician.

If you decide to get a rocker, the newest thing is the glider. Unlike the arch-shaped runners that tilt traditional rockers back and forth, the glider is on a pedestal that moves the chair forward and backward on a smooth, even plane. This makes for a very comfortable motion when you're nursing or trying to get the baby to nod off. Gliders also add a dimension of safety, since you won't have to worry about nipping little fingers or toes under the runners, though fingers can get caught in the slider mechanism. Glider rockers used to be very ugly, with hideous cushion covers in awful coarse fabrics that looked like the drapes at the Department of Motor Vehicles. Now gliders come in enough different styles that you should be able to find something that will look fine in the nursery and might even look like a traditional rocker.

Fortunately, many stores let you select fabric for custom-made slipcovers. You can match your nursery decor and then later you can have a different cover made in a fabric that reflects your child's interest in decor.

Of course, a good old-fashioned rocker still does the trick and it's a terrific thing to borrow from someone. Just make sure you have enough padding to make it comfortable.

Chair comfort is very subjective, so take a lesson from Goldilocks and try every one until you find one that's "just right." The armrests should be at a comfortable height. Some chairs have padded armrests, but if you're after aesthetics you might prefer using a pillow under your arm.

Your Budget

Dutalier is the most popular manufacturer of glider rockers. If aesthetics are not an issue, you can purchase a glider for as little as $180, but they go up to $500. Dutalier also makes gliding ottomans that match the chairs ($120 to $150). I recommend trying the ottoman before purchasing, because the motion of the ottoman and the chair together can make some people queasy. You might prefer a stationary ottoman or none at all.

Shermag, another popular brand of gliders, offers chairs that are less expensive than Dutalier but with fewer fabric and style choices. You might be asking yourself, why would one glider be $179 and another be $399? Just like with cribs, price has more to do with style than function. The more expensive chairs generally have thicker cushions for comfort, and padded arms, and may be taller and wider, but as I said earlier, you'll have to park your butt in as many different chairs as you can to see which one is most comfortable for you. Another tip: When you're shopping for these while pregnant, remember that you won't be this large later on in life (hopefully), so don't stress if you feel a little squished. Also, get Daddy to do some chair tests because, first, he may do the 2 a.m. feeding in this chair, and second, this chair might end up in a den later.

If you have it in your head that you want a traditional

rocker, you might find one at a garage sale, in a North Carolina furniture factory, or at any furniture store. Just get what you like.

Baby Monitor

- Might Want
- Birth to out of crib
- Good to borrow
- Price range: $30 to $350

A BABY MONITOR is a one-way walkie-talkie system that you use to keep an ear on your baby when you are at the other end of the house. You put the monitor's transmitting end in the baby's room, and keep the receiving end with you, so if the baby starts to cry you can run to him in an instant (unless you're practicing the Ferber Method, and then the baby's cries will only serve to torture you). I've heard some cute stories and some horror stories about people picking up unwanted phone conversations (some more interesting than others) on their baby monitors. This is more of a problem in an apartment building than in a house. At any rate, you need a baby monitor to hear your baby when you're in a different room.

If you live in a busy city, you may get a lot of interference from cellular phones, taxi dispatchers, fire stations, truck drivers, and anyone else using a radio. For this reason, never throw out the box that your baby monitor comes in. For whatever reason, certain monitors work better in certain locations than others. My philosophy is to buy the cheapest one first and see if it does the job. If it does, great. If it doesn't, pack it up in the box and bring it back to trade in for the next level. Always save the monitor's original package, because many stores won't take returns without them. Also keep in mind that two from the same company don't always work identically.

I suggest purchasing a baby monitor in a big chain store. Monitors are often used as a "loss leaders," which are items that the store offers at cost, hoping to lure shoppers in to buy other products. Check Sunday circulars for sales on baby monitors.

If you're planning on having a nurse when you come home from the hospital who will be sleeping in the baby's room, you won't need a monitor until she leaves.

It Must Have

❑ The parent's unit should be able to run on **battery, as well as with an AC adapter** to give you the convenience of portability but not cost you a fortune in batteries.

If You're Borrowing

If you are lucky enough to be able to borrow a baby monitor, check it to see if it works. If it does, grab it.

Your Budget

Start out on the low end and upgrade only if the lowest–end product doesn't work for you. The most budget-conscious baby monitor available and the most popular is the Fisher-Price Sound & Lights Monitor ($19.99). As the name suggests, this also has a light display. A unique feature is that both transmitting and receiving end will work on battery or electric power, so you can take it when you travel or use it in a huge backyard. In the $30 to $50 range is the Safety 1st Clear Connection, the Graco UltraClear Monitor and the First Years Crisp and Clear Plus. Note that the word "clear" is prevalent in the naming of these products.

For the truly neurotic, you guessed it, the video monitor is here. The official name is the Safety 1st Child View Monitor and Television ($150). This wireless audio/video monitor is not to spy on your babysitter, but to watch with amazement as your baby's tummy moves up and down in slumber. What makes this even more nifty is that the monitor converts to an actual television so when you tire of watching your baby's breathing patterns, you can flip a switch and catch up on *All My Children*.

Layette

THE LAYETTE CONSISTS of clothing, bedding, bathing paraphernalia, and little odds and ends that you will need when the baby first comes home. Think of furniture as the hardware and the layette items as the "software." Every store you go into and every book you read will have a "layette list." They will all be different. The reason? Everyone has their own opinion and you will too. Will you and your baby be fine if you have four receiving blankets instead of eight? A nail clipper instead of a nail scissors? Plain white crib sheets or color–coordinated ones? Your layette should consist of the items that you will need for your baby. My advice is not to go overboard too far in advance—you'll have a much better idea of what you need two weeks after the birth than in your last trimester.

Virtually everything that follows is a Must Have, no matter what your budget level. Unless you're playing a personal game of "Survivor" and you can make do with palm leaf diapers and nail clippers made from sharpened rocks, you'll need most of these items to keep a baby happy, healthy, and clean. No one item is particularly expensive, but they do add up in the end. Just keep thinking of all the money you'll save by never going to the movies anymore.

My general advice about purchasing clothing is to buy very few items in the beginning. Don't buy fourteen snap-shirts and fourteen onesies (don't worry, I'll explain what these things are). Once you try them you'll develop a preference for what is easier for you to use. Also, you don't know how quickly the baby will grow. Yes, Baby Gap has all that adorable stuff, but save your money until Melissa can wear things long enough for you to get a picture of her in them and for you to amortize the cost with a few visits to show them off. As for size, I recommend purchasing size Small as opposed to Newborn—baby will get a bit more wear out of these outfits even if they might seem a little baggy at first. Let people who don't know any better get you all the outfits in Newborn size, because it will kill you to buy outfits that get worn once and are too small the next time you try them on. Also keep in mind that the size labels on baby clothes are erratic, to say the least. Babies' bodies vary so much and they grow so fast that clothing sizes can't be as precise as for adults. It's very likely that your child will fit into different articles of clothing labeled for sizes anywhere from 6 months to 18 months.

If you've read the chapter on borrowing, you know that I'm not big on borrowing clothes. There are too many possibilities of ruining things. Of course, if someone has lots of Onesies and the like that were used for just a few months, are in good shape, and are being offered on a nonreturnable basis, they're worth a look. Much of the baby's time these first few months will be spent in the house, in your arms or in the bassinet, so unless Grandma or Aunt Sophie and Uncle Mel are coming by, wearing a used snapshirt will not be a problem and may actually be preferable, considering the volume of spit-up that is possible at this stage. As for a layette's odds and ends, would you want to borrow someone else's nail clippers or baby thermometer? Enough said.

Snapshirt

- Might Want
- Birth to 12 months
- Bad to borrow
- Price: 2 for $6.29

SNAPSHIRTS ARE T-SHIRTS that snap on the side so they don't have to be put on over the baby's head. This is useful

Snapshirt

because infants tend not to like having things pulled over their heads. They also come in long sleeves with mittens to prevent the baby from scratching himself with those razor-sharp finger-nails. Parents also prefer these in the beginning, before the umbilical cord has fallen off, because they're open on the bottom and loose-fitting and therefore won't knock the cord off prematurely. They come in solid white and prints. Carter's is one popular manufacturer. I would recommend starting with **four in the 3-month size** and **four in the 6-month size** (two packages of each).

Onesies

- Might Want
- Birth to 2 years
- Bad to borrow
- Price: $4.99

ONESIES RESEMBLE BABY leotards. They are a one-piece undershirts that snap in between the baby's legs. The generic term for this garment is really bodysuit, but like Vaseline and Kleenex, Onesie has become the adopted name. A onesie gives baby a more pulled-together look because the item snaps down over the diaper and stays tucked in better. These are made by Carter's and Gerber, and I recommend starting with **three in size Small** and **three in size Medium.** Most parents choose to go with a

> ▶ **TIP:** When you launder baby clothes, place them inside a net bag so you won't lose any of the tiny things in the washing machine.

Onesie

combination of snap-shirts and onesies. You'll probably develop a preference over time.

Gown

- Might Want
- Birth to 3 months
- Bad to borrow
- Price range: $6.99 to $26.99

FEDERAL LAWS MAKE it necessary for any item sold as sleep-wear to be of flame-retardant materials like polyester. A polyester infant nightgown with an elastic hem to keep the feet covered retails for about $6.99. The advantage of a gown is that you don't have to force the baby's feet into the separate legs with attached booties, which can be a pain for the both of you. These garments are closed at the bottom, but there's plenty of room for babies to move their feet and legs. There are imported "two-way playsuits" in cotton, whose packaging states that they are "not intended for sleepwear." You can either snap the bottom together to create a bag of sorts, or snap the sides separately to create legs. Many parents use these as gowns. They retail for about $26.99. In cooler months, some people use a similar garment made of a fleece fabric, called an infant sleeping bag ($13.99).

Stretchy

- Must Have
- Birth to 2 years
- Bad to borrow
- Price range: $8.99 to $25

THIS IS A one-piece pajama with snaps down the entire front opening and down one leg. For $8.99 you can get the flame-retardant terry type with feet (Carter's Terry Stretchy). There are cotton ones without feet—again, known as "playsuits"—for $10.99, and high-end imports with feet in cotton for $25 (manufactured by Sarah's Prints and Mini Basix). I recommend that you start with **three in size Small** and **three in size Medium.**

Blanket Sleeper

- Might Want
- 6 months to 4 years
- Bad to borrow
- Price: $11.99 to $15.99

THIS IS A fuzzy, warm Dr. Denton–type pajama in a poly-fleece fabric, the same fabric used in the infant sleeping bag, but with feet for when the baby is older. If you recall, the blanket sleeper is similar to the "feetsy" pajamas that we used to wear as kids with the plastic soles that went swish swish on the linoleum kitchen floor. Carter's, as you may have guessed, also manufactures these garments. You don't need to purchase blanket sleepers as part of your initial layette because **the baby won't use them until six months,** but you should probably have **two or three for baby's**

first winter after six months, if you live in a cold climate and have a drafty home.

Cloth Diapers

- Must Have
- Birth to when they move out (good for dusting)
- Bad to borrow
- Price: $21.99 per dozen

EVEN IF YOU'VE decided to go disposable, stock up with a dozen cloth diapers. Go for the prefolded ones because they're padded in the middle. It doesn't matter what brand.

What will you do with them? You'll wear them over your shoulder for at least the first six months for burping. You'll wipe a broad variety of baby-created and baby-instigated messes off of every family member, including the baby, without buying stock in Bounty or using scratchy dish towels or HandiWipes. You'll roll them up and support the baby's head in the car seat. You'll tie Cheerios in them. You'll lose them and not get depressed. They're indispensable.

Hat

- Must Have
- Birth to 3 months
- Bad to borrow
- Price range: $2.99 to $6.99

YOU'LL PROBABLY GET one of these at the hospital, but you'll want a few more around the house for those first trips outside. There are cute hats with ear flaps that look like aviation helmets and have a chin string, or you can get a cotton knit hat that fits snugly without a chin string, which makes many parents more comfortable because they think the string could choke the baby (it probably won't, but you might be more comfortable without it).

Booties

- Must Have
- Birth to 6 months
- Bad to borrow
- Price: $2.99

THESE ARE TINY cotton socks. They must have an elastic band knitted into the top or they will not stay on tiny baby feet. I recommend purchasing several pairs, all in the same color, because you will most likely lose some of these. You should **start with three pairs,** and if you want you can break down and go to Baby Gap, where you can find them in 15 happening colors.

Receiving Blankets

- Must Have
- Birth to 2 years
- Bad to borrow
- Price range: $6.99 to $19.99

A RECEIVING BLANKET is a thin, 100 percent cotton (sometimes thermal cotton, sometimes flannel) blanket that you will use constantly during the first several months of your baby's life. What distinguishes it from other blankets is a very soft, thin fabric with an open weave (so you don't have to worry about suffocation if it inadvertently covers the baby's face). Many manufacturers make receiving blankets. The most popular are the cotton thermal blankets that are both warm in the winter and cool in the summer. Don't be alarmed by their texture when you touch them in the packaging—the fabric becomes much softer after washing. Receiving blankets are generally 36-inch squares. There are fancy imported models with a finer weave that are larger and are sometimes embroidered. You will use receiving blankets in the bassinet or crib instead of a regular blanket, which can be too heavy, in a stroller instead of a wool blanket in warm weather, or to swaddle the baby after a bath or when going outside. **Get four to six.**

Hooded towels

- Might Want
- Birth to 12 months
- Bad to borrow
- Price range: $6.99 to $19.99

THESE ARE NICE to wrap the baby in after a bath. They don't have any use beyond that, so the expensive, decorated ones that go for $19.99 or more and that make your kid look like a duck or a dog aren't worth it to me unless they're irresistible to you. **Get two to four** of these. You should be able to get them for around $6.99 apiece. By the way, any towel, even one with, heaven forbid, NO HOOD, will do just fine. These just have a finer weave that makes them somewhat softer than your towels.

Washcloths

- Might Want
- Birth to 12 months
- Bad to borrow
- Price: 2 for $2.99

THESE MAY SEEM like a luxury, but baby washcloths are smaller and softer than the ones you use, made of a tighter weave and without the plushness that works for you but which would be rougher for the baby. You could probably raise a healthy, happy baby without using these, but at two for $2.99, **buy six.** You'll do baby's skin a favor, and you'll be doing yourself a favor at bath time when your kid's more cooperative because of them.

Another part of the layette is bedding. If you are planning on using a bassinet for the first three months, then your initial layette purchases will include the bassinet size for some of these items. The crib bedding can wait until you're ready. The following are in order of necessity.

Waterproof Sheet

- Must Have
- Birth to accidents stop happening
- Bad to borrow
- Price: Bassinet size—$5.99 Crib size—$10.99

THIS IS THE RUBBER liner that directly covers the mattress. Waterproof sheets are available in flat or fitted styles. I recommend flat, since this sheet will be covered by the fitted quilted pad. Fitted ones are twice the price.

Even though you'll have diapered baby to within an inch of his life, the sheets may still get damp, so you'll need these. **Buy two** of these—there's a good chance one will be wet.

> ▶ **TIP:** Parents used to complain that formula stains were impossible to get out. Not anymore. There is a non-toxic stain remover called Mother's Little Miracle (sexist name, great product) that gets out spit up, urine, vomit and potty training accident odors and stains. If you still want to be a parent after reading this list, pick up a bottle of it for $4.99.

Quilted Pads

- Must Have
- Birth to out of crib
- Bad to borrow
- Price: Bassinets size—$5.99 Crib size—$11.99 to $19.99

THIS IS THE LAYER that goes over the waterproof sheet to make the bed softer and cooler. Without pads, you'll have your baby sleeping on the sheet and the rubber liner, and I doubt that you want that. They are available in a flat style with two anchor bands ($11.99), or in a fitted style ($14.99), which stays on better and is a bit easier to handle. I recommend getting **two,** whichever style you choose.

There are combinations of the two above items available, but you should avoid these. They are rubberized on the inside and therefore cannot be fully dried in the dryer. Often if the baby wets the bed, nothing reaches the bottom waterproof sheet layer anyway. In these cases you could wash and thoroughly dry a regular quilted pad more conveniently than waiting for the combination type to air dry.

Crib Sheets

- Must Have
- Birth to twin bed
- Bad to borrow
- Price: Bassinet size—$4.99 to $8.99
         Crib size—$8.99 to $35

YOU WILL NEED four sheets (two for bassinets)—I recommend getting **at least two in plain white cotton.** Carter's makes a crib sheet for $8.99, and Crib Critters makes a sheet that is cut more generously for $14.99. You'll want that extra room, as cotton tends to shrink. You can get one or two sheets to match your bumper set for when company is coming, but these run at least $20 each, depending on how crazy you go on your bedding. You will change these sheets all the time, so basically you will use as many sheets as you have. Knit ones, as opposed to combed cotton, are easier to put on, plus you don't have to iron them, so they're softer on your baby's face. Don't knock yourself out trying to find a flat cover sheet like you have on your own bed. They're not made in this country.

Bumper

- Must Have
- Birth to baby uses it to climb out of the crib
- Bad to borrow
- Price range: $35 to you name it

THIS IS THE LAST Must Have on the list. The bumper is the padding that goes around the inside walls of the crib and it's a Must Have because it will keep your baby from smacking his head against the slats of the crib. There are two style choices—the four-sided or the headboard bumper. The four-sided is a basic bumper that goes around the crib at one height (10 to 12 inches). The "Hollywood Headboard," as I like to call it, has a padded piece at the head of the crib that is taller and rounded. Unless you like the look, you shouldn't get it—it's more expensive and it doesn't provide any extra safety for the baby (and it usually comes with an ugly appliqué). In the aesthetics department, you have a choice of a ruffle or piping edge on the whole bumper. More expensive bumpers offer the option of channel stitching, which creates a puckered fabric effect. Many people want cotton but this is overrated; poly/cotton will suffice because the baby does not sleep on the bumper. The filling of all bumpers is flame-retardant.

The price can go from $35 for a simple, solid-colored bumper to an obscene $200, but the average range is $60 to $80. I tell my customers not to get too crazy about the bumper because you will be lucky to keep it in the crib for a year before the baby starts to use it as a step stool to climb out of the crib. Budget-conscious brands are Kids Line, Sumersault, Glenna Jean, Quiltex, and Lambs and Ivy. Midpriced manufacturers include NoJo, and Cotton Tales Patchkraft, and high-end manufacturers include Pine Creek, Sleeping Partners, Navas Designs, and Laura Ashley. Some sellers, littlelinens.com, for example, will customize bumpers.

There are two ways to fasten the bumper to the sides of the crib. Some bumpers tie only on the top and some tie on both top and bottom. The manufacturers can justify their particular method, but you should consult your pediatrician for the last word. The top/bottom people claim that it prevents baby from wedging his head under the bumper. The top-only people claim that if baby wedges his head, he can't get as stuck as he could with the top/bottom bumper. Make sure you follow the washing instructions carefully.

Crib Bib

- Might Want
- Birth to end of the spit-ups
- Bad to borrow
- Price: 2 for $15.99

THIS IS A piece of fabric that goes under the baby's head while he sleeps so that if he spits up you don't have to change the whole sheet. It comes in cotton terry or flannel and goes all the way across the sheet to where the baby's head is. There are ties that fasten the item on the slats of the crib to keep it in place. Our parents used cloth diapers for this purpose and so can you. I would save the money.

Dust Ruffle

- Might Want
- Birth to out of crib
- Bad to borrow
- Price range: $30 to $100

OUNCE FOR OUNCE, this is the most expensive piece of bedding. The dust ruffle really serves no purpose. It goes underneath the mattress and hangs down on all four sides to hide the hardware and springs under the crib. That's it. Most people get them anyway. Again, people are obsessed with getting a ruffle in cotton, but it is even less important here because the baby never touches it. I can see why you might obsess over the sheets and the bumper, but once you begin to worry about matching dust ruffles and comforters, you're starting to lose me.

Comforter

- Totally Optional
- Bad to borrow
- Price range: $40 to $200

COMFORTERS ARE TOO heavy for a newborn. You might want one, but you'll probably end up using it as a wall hanging, or to drape over the side of the crib, or as a cushion on the floor for baby to lie on. If you want a decorative blanket that you can really use, have Aunt Audrey crochet an afghan full of nice, lacy holes that will let baby breathe in case he pulls it over his head. The more expensive ones are cotton, could have a patchwork or reversible design, and can be custom–made. The manufacturers usually make bumpers, too. Some bedding companies are getting smart and making thin blankets to match the newborn bed sets to tempt you to buy both blanket and comforter. I can tell you that in many cases their wishes are coming true.

Keep in mind that you can go a few weeks without bedding. Classic pink and blue still define a baby's world. If you don't know the sex of your baby and don't want to opt for unisex pastels like yellow or mint green, hold off. If your newborn sleeps in a bassinet, you have eight weeks. If you are ordering bedding, it usually only takes two to three weeks to arrive. Some companies sell complete sets (bumper, quilt, sheet, and dust ruffle) that you can get immediately. Some baby stores have relationships with companies that allow you to provide fabric for the bedding. This is a great parent pleaser because bedding can be completely suited to your own taste. If you are pressed for space and need to use the nursery as a guest room, you can make up the guest bed in a matching fabric. You can also match your rocking chair's cushion to the bedding.

Don't bother purchasing bedding with the second child in mind (like buying something unisex, just in case). The bedding will get ruined or you will discover something about it that you don't like by the time the second child arrives. Also, follow the instructions when washing comforters because the filling inside can get lumpy and misshapen.

There are also several other items that you will need to keep your baby happy, healthy, and clean.

Pacifiers

- Must Have
- Birth to thumb awareness
- Unthinkable to borrow
- Price range: $1.99 to $2.99

EVEN IF YOU don't believe in using pacifiers, you might want to bring a couple home anyway. You might change your mind after four or five hours of nonstop crying. If you have questions about the politics of pacifiers, talk to your pediatrician. Two of the most popular brands are Nuk by Gerber (two for $3.99) and Mini Mam by Sassy (two for $4.99). These are both orthodontic pacifiers, which means that they are shaped flat and wide like a natural nipple. A reason that I recommend the most popular brands is that if your child becomes addicted to pacifiers, you want to be able to pick up a spare at any locale. Since you don't know what kind your baby will like, I suggest trying a pack of each.

Pacifier Clip

- Might Want
- Birth to thumb awareness
- Bad to borrow
- Price: $3.99

THIS BRILLIANT ITEM snaps onto the baby's clothes and dangles the pacifier at the other end. This is a good thing to have, unless you like the idea of bending over and picking up a dropped pacifier hundreds of times a day, not to mention washing it off after it's fallen on the street and bounced once or twice. The one warning here is to never attach this to your baby in the crib, as it can pose a strangulation hazard.

Pacifier Case

- Might Want
- As long as you have pacifiers
- Bad to borrow
- Price: $2.99

LIKE THE HOLDER above, this is the sort of thing that you wouldn't think existed but you'll be really happy to have. This is just a little, snap-open plastic case, shaped sort of like a space capsule, to protect the pacifier when baby's not using it. The pacifier stays clean, and you'll have a better-than-average chance of finding it when you need it.

Baby Manicure Set

- Must Have
- Birth to self-grooming
- Bad to borrow
- Price: $5.99 and up

BABIES GROW SURPRISINGLY fast, and their fingernails seem to grow the fastest. It seems like they need to be cut daily or baby will give herself little cuts on her face that will make you feel like one of the worst parents alive. Cutting baby's nails is not easy; some parents report that it's best to wait until the baby is asleep. Whenever you do it, you'll need a manicure set, with a tiny clipper, a tiny scissors, and a tiny emery board. In the beginning it is easiest to cut baby's nails with the scissors. Revlon makes a nice individual infant scissors for $7.99. You can buy all three items together from First Years for $5.99.

Thermometer

- Must Have
- Birth to preschool age
- Bad to borrow
- Price range: $3.99 to $79.99

AS I'M SURE you know, babies have their temperature taken in a different way from older kids and adults. This is historically one of the more unpleasant jobs of being a parent, made even more of a struggle because taking a baby's rectal temperature is never easy, both you and the baby will probably be upset when you have to take it, and it's not something that, frankly, you get to practice a lot. Ask your pediatrician about the hows and whys; I

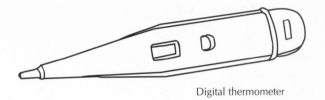

Digital thermometer

can only assure you that a regular rectal thermometer is a little less harrowing than you may remember; the bulb is quite small, and in the opinion of most parents and doctors I know, it remains the best way to take a baby's temperature.

For a long time it was the only way to take a baby's temperature, until the recent invention of digital thermometers and the Thermoscan. A digital thermometer works the same way a regular rectal one does, except that the readout is displayed in numbers and you don't have to think about glass and mercury. It can be either oral or rectal. As for the Thermoscan, well, you might have already had some conversations about it. A handheld, battery-operated tool, it's about the size and shape of an electric toothbrush. To use it, you put a disposable cover on top of the probe end, insert it gently into the ear canal to create a seal, and then press the button on top for one second. The temperature readout is then shown digitally on the handle. Sounds great, doesn't it? But there's a lot a discussion among doctors and other professionals as to how accurate it is for newborns, so before you take the leap, talk to your pediatrician. You don't want to play around here; fevers during the first three months are treated with extreme caution.

Prices range from $3.99 for a standard thermometer, $9.99 for a digital one, and $79.99 for a Thermoscan. Even if you get a Thermoscan, I'd still get a rectal thermometer, just in case.

Nasal Aspirator

- Must Have
- Birth to self nose blowing
- Bad to borrow
- Price: $2.99

THIS IS THE thing that resembles a miniature turkey baster. It extracts mucous from the baby's nose in lieu of blowing (which they don't get the hang of until much later in life). You may never use it, but you'll still want to have it around just in case, especially if your baby is born during the fall or winter.

nasal aspirator

Comb/Brush

- Must Have
- Birth to premature balding
- Bad to borrow
- Price: $3.99 and up

EVEN IF BABY has no hair, it's good to brush the peach fuzz on their heads to massage the scalp and for hygiene. Before you buy a brush, feel the bristles to make sure they're soft to the touch. You can get a simple brush and comb set for $3.99 to $7.99, or, for you Rockefellers, Tiffany's sells sterling silver sets for boys at $265 and for girls at $415.

First Aid Book

- Must Have
- Bad to borrow
- Price: $14.95 or so

THIS IS A GOOD thing to have around. Ask your pediatrician which first aid book she recommends. When you flip through it, you might start to think that there is virtually no way to keep the baby alive for more than a week, but relax and put it back on the shelf for when you need it. At that point, it will be a great comfort. Still, it's not a substitute for taking a lifesaving class.

As to all the drugstore items like lotions, cleansers, wipes, swabs, cotton balls, and such, follow your pediatrician's recommendations.

Bathtub

- Must Have
- About 2 weeks to 1 year
- Okay to borrow
- Price range: $13.99 to $45

Essentials
▶ Drain plug
▶ Nonskid surface

A BATHTUB IS simply a basin, nine or so inches deep with a sloped back, in which you wash your baby. When new parents look for a bathtub, they often want something nice and snug that fits in the sink. If they find such a thing, which isn't easy—especially if they live in a small apartment with an equally small sink—they'll soon be back at the store buying a bigger one because the baby will outgrow it in a matter of months. About the only good thing to say about a small baby tub is that it's easier to store than a bigger one. As you can tell, I recommend bigger baby bathtubs. Unless you buy a Bathinette, the biggest tub will still fit on top of the changing table, the baby won't soon grow out of it, and once the baby is more active and almost sitting up, you can place the baby tub within your own bathtub. This is a plus because you don't have to scrub your tub every night to remove Daddy's hair, which at this point is probably coming out in clumps. Most doctors recommend that you give your baby sponge baths until the umbilical cord falls off; then you can start with full baths.

There may be some of you that feel you can manage without a baby tub, simply using the sink or tub with an insert. After one session with a wriggly, soapy baby with hard faucets and four inches of water in which he can easily drown if you don't hold on, you might change your mind and buy a tub.

It Must Have

❏ It should have a **drain plug** because it is easier to drain the water than to dump it out of the top. This also makes it easier to clean out.
❏ The tub should also have **a nonskid surface** to prevent baby's tushy from sliding. Some people prefer to buy a large bath sponge (approximately $7) for the baby to sit on, but I'm not totally convinced. While a sponge can keep the baby from slipping and also cradle him and keep him warmer, they don't dry quickly and can become mildewed. If you use a sponge and it begins to fall apart, immediately replace it: Those little bits of sponge are choking hazards disguised as extremely tempting snacks.

If You're Borrowing

This isn't the first thing I'd try to borrow; it's just a plastic

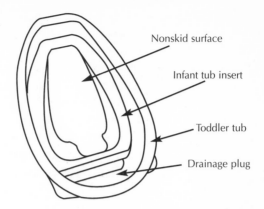

Nonskid surface

Infant tub insert

Toddler tub

Drainage plug

basin, and you can get a perfectly good one for a couple of dollars more than a can of powdered formula. But if you insist, make sure the nonskid surface is intact, the plug fully seals the drain, and there are no cracks in the plastic.

Your Budget

Bathtubs are generally not very expensive, so you should purchase one that best suits your needs. Given that a baby tub is essentially a plastic bowl, it's hard to believe that some tout various features, but maybe one of them will sound good to you. For instance, the Safety 1st Infant Bath Tub ($11.99) has an angled back rest that cradles the baby's head. Graco Cuddle Tub ($19.99) has a little hammock made of mesh netting that the baby sits in, though I've gotten complaints that the hammock keeps the baby too far out of the water. My personal favorite in this category is the Evenflo Infant Toddler Bath ($19.99). This is really a tub within a tub because it has a firm insert lined with an eigth-inch sponged, which then snaps into the bigger bathtub. The insert can be used on its own as a small tub for bathing an infant in a sink. The Evenflo also has the widest interior, making it easier to maneuver your baby. Another good choice in a tub that is usable from birth through toddler age is the Safety 1st 4-In-One Bath Station ($19.99). This is a tub with a detatchable sling and bath ring. When the baby is a newborn, you can use the sling directly in the sink. When he's a bit bigger but not sitting up, you can use the sling to support him in the tub. At around six months and sitting up, the bath ring is used in the tub and once he is secure enough without the bath ring, the tub is used on its own.

There are portable bathtubs that are good for travel. The Fold-up Tub, by Safety 1st ($12.99), for example, has two cupped sides that fold up over a center bowl. People in apartments also like this tub because it folds up so small.

Another popular bathing item is the Bathinette (just say bassinet with a lisp and you've got it). It looks like a changing table, but when you flip up the top, there's a bathtub inside. This setup has several pluses: First, you can change, bathe, and dress the baby all in one convenient, space-saving location. Second, the Bathinette is on wheels, so you can move it easily. Third, eventually the tub comes out and it will become a dresser. There are some drawbacks. Most immediately, you must use the Bathinette in the kitchen or bathroom (which somewhat negates the convenience of dressing the baby there), the water-bailing process is somewhat annoying; you have to empty the soapy water, replace with clean water for rinsing the baby, and then empty it all via a hose in the back. Also, the drawers are cheaply made, and the Bathinette is not something you would want to keep as furniture once the baby gets older. However, it is relatively inexpensive. There is one style with drawers for $199 and one with open shelves underneath for $129. Made by Brevi, Bathinettes are imported from Italy.

Bath Seat

- Must Have
- 6 months till you have to soap the baby to fit him in
- Okay to borrow
- Price range: $13.99 to $18.99

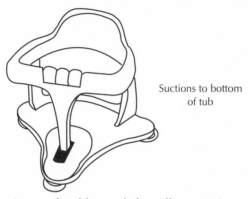

Suctions to bottom
of tub

AT FIVE OR six months old, your baby will start sitting up and many things will change, not the least of which will be bath time. Unless yours is a water baby, bath time at this point can be an adventure somewhere between octopus wrestling and fishing for pike with your bare hands. A bath seat will help you control Junior in the tub while he is splashing, and squirming, and trying to drink the bath water. Basically, it is a big plastic ring attached to a seat base, with suction cups to secure it to the tub floor. Take note: suction cups will not stick to nonskid surfaces. Another drawback is that you'll have to work a little harder to wash the tushy. Once again, bath seats are relatively inexpensive items—under $20—so budgeting is not a concern. Get what you like.

Safety First

The Consumer Products Safety Commission has a special

recorded message about bath seats. It's a cautionary tale about parents who left their baby in a bath seat while they went to answer the door. When they came back, the baby had drowned. A bath seat is not a flotation device—NEVER LEAVE YOUR CHILD UNATTENDED IN THE BATH!

If You're Borrowing

Again, not a prime choice for borrowing, but if you do, be sure that all the suction cups are there and in good shape.

Your Budget

The Safety 1st Swivel Bath Seat ($8.99) has some nice features. As you may have guessed, the seat swivels so that you can move the baby around with one hand and get to the hard-to-reach places. It has big suction cups, all the better to stick bath seats securely to tubs. The Swivel Bath Seat also has a beaded toy in the front which is sure to captivate baby for about eight seconds.

The Fisher-Price Stay n' Play bath ring ($18.99) has the widest seat for baby's tushy. The bottom is designed like a bathtub mat, with many suction cups, giving it the best sticking surface of all of these.

Bathing Accessories

As you can imagine, there are loads of accessories for the bath. I'll just mention some that my customers have found useful.

The Bather Saver ($16.99)—This is a plastic cushioned pad that goes over the side of the tub. The purpose is to save the knees and elbows of the parent (a.k.a. the "bather") who is kneeling on the hard bathroom tile with elbows leaning on the hard porcelain tub while administering a bath to a bathee.

The Bath Saver Mat ($10.99)—This bathtub mat with an elephant illustration goes on the bottom of the tub in place of a regular bath mat. If the water is too hot, the elephant changes colors. Another water temperature gauge is a floating **Ducky thermometer** ($2.99). You can always substitute your finger (free of charge).

The Tubbly Bubbly ($14.99)—A hard rubber sleeve shaped like an elephant trunk slips over the bathtub spout. You can pour bubble bath into the trunk, and bubbles will come out with the bath water. Everyone who has ever bathed with a sibling can appreciate this product—one always wound up smacking his head on the spoutend of the tub. As the youngest of four, I can tell you it's not fun. Along the same lines is an **inflatable spout/knob protector** ($3.99, but sorry, no bubbles).

Sprayer nozzle ($5.99)—Safety 1st and First Years both make ones that fit on the end of the water spout. This is useful for rinsing out shampoo, and many babies enjoy the sprayed water. One hitch: they don't fit every nozzle. When you purchase one, don't rip open the box because you may have to return it. In lieu of a sprayer, you might prefer to use a simple plastic pitcher to rinse your baby.

Rubber visor ($4.99)—The Eyes are Dry visor helps keep water and shampoo out of eyes while rinsing. Some parents have told me that this is useful to keep the baby's ear dry during an infection. Otherwise, put one on your child's head and tell me that you're proud.

Toys—Check out some inventive bath toys on the market: Sort of like color forms, bath time stickers that stick to the wall when wet are big sellers. They come in alphabet letters, numbers, farm animals, and cowboys. Another nice idea, if Baby Jane fusses about having her face washed, is a sponge puppet ($6.99). They're available in dragons, cows, and frogs, and endless other variations. And of course, when all else fails, there is the rubber duck ($2.99).

Bath Toy Bag ($5.99)—You may need a place to store all of these toys when you or another adult wants to use the tub and shower facility. The answer is the Bath Toy Bag, which is a mesh bag that attaches to the wall with suction cups.

Carriages and Strollers

THE SELECTION OF a stroller ranks somewhere between the amnio and the first Lamaze class on most new parents' anxiety meter. But relax! The first stroller you purchase (most likely a carriage/stroller) will not be your last, so don't obsess over it. While the stroller provides everyday transportation for your baby, the decision doesn't need to be as complicated as buying a new car. The only "right" carriage or stroller is the one that works for you. I've said this before, but it's especially true here. You're going to be weighing a lot of variables, so think about how you'll be using the stroller instead of buying it based solely on features that may have no real value to you.

The first question people often ask is, "What's the difference between a carriage and a stroller?" In short, the baby faces you in a carriage and faces away from you in a stroller. With that settled, the three main types of products in the stroller category are the pram, the carriage/stroller, and the umbrella stroller. A pram is the beautiful, stately-looking carriage with big white wheels that you would expect to see Mary Poppins pushing around in some London garden. As you can imagine, prams are not terribly practical, but I'll go into that in the next section. The carriage/stroller is, as the name implies, convertible to either a stroller or a carriage via a reversible handle. This is the most practical approach however carriage/strollers are becoming a dying breed, making way for an ever-growing selection of travel systems. The umbrella stroller is the second stroller. When parents get sick of lugging around a heavier carriage/stroller, they move to an umbrella stroller. This is a much lighter, more compact stroller that can be used after a child is around three months old.

When you are shopping for a stroller or carriage, you

should keep the primary user in mind and make sure that the stroller will be comfortable for that person. Ideally, the primary user, like your baby-sitter, should be stroller shopping with you. The main comfort factor is height. A taller person needs a higher handle for comfort. This is very important; it becomes very annoying very quickly to push a stroller that is too low. Another comfort factor is stride. If the primary user has a particularly long stride, they might kick the wheels. You should experiment around the store before your purchase. Finally, there's weight. Heaving the stroller up and down stairs is bad enough, but as the baby gets bigger, simply pushing a heavy stroller can become a strain. Keep Mommy's, Daddy's, or nanny's lower lumbar region in mind when making this purchase.

Another important consideration is where you live. If you live in an urban area, you'll probably be walking every day on city streets and sidewalks and for relatively long distances. You'll definitely want something that's lightweight, durable and convenient both to push and to store. Does your building have a lot of steps in the front? Do you live in a walk-up? Dragging a heavy stroller up and down might feel heroic the first time or two, but a week later you'll be buying a lighter stroller. Incidentally, the more expensive strollers tend to be lighter. They are made from lighter-weight, more expensive metals, and involve more sophisticated engineering.

If you live in the suburbs and go from car to shopping cart, or if your stroller will only touch mall floors, durability won't matter as much. I know people who use the least expensive (unofficially referred to as "disposable") strollers for their young kids and replace them as needed. Since it won't get as much use as an urban stroller, cost will probably be more of a factor, as will convenience. To store the stroller or put it in the trunk of your car, you must fold it. This can be a simple procedure or a nightmare. Don't take anyone's word on the ease of folding a stroller—master this task before leaving the store with your purchase. You must also keep in mind that you will often be holding the baby as you fold the stroller, so it should be easy to do as a one-hand operation.

I recommend highly purchasing a stroller from a reputable store. If the stroller needs repair (and it will), a good store might provide you with a loaner unit. This is very important because you can't be without a stroller for the several weeks it may take to repair yours.

In the end, you simply have to purchase what will be comfortable and workable for your particular lifestyle.

Pram/Carriage

- Totally Optional
- Birth to 6 months
- Good to borrow
- Price range: $299 to $1,500

Essentials
▶ Basket

IF YOU LIVE in the city, a pram is not a very convenient item. It is very bulky and difficult to navigate through narrow store aisles. They don't fold, so in addition to a nanny in a starched white uniform to push the thing, you will need a Range Rover or some other such vehicle to transport it. In fact, no matter where you live, a pram is not a very convenient item.

But prams are not about convenience; they're about luxury. If you've ever dreamed of pushing a baby buggy, you've dreamed about pushing a pram, and they're worth dreaming about. You can't beat prams for aesthetics, with their shiny frames, big hoods, and wheels.

There are other advantages, too. Your newborn can sleep in comfort in a pram because it has its own mattress, which can be made up with waterproof sheets and easily cleaned. A pram can be used in lieu of a bassinet, and some even have a removable basket. Because a pram has spring suspension, it is easy to rock an agitated baby to sleep, and the pram is higher off the ground than any other carriage, making it easier to get the baby in and out. In cold weather, it is easier to bundle the baby in the pram, and, in summer, the larger hood is the best at blocking the sun.

So what's the problem?

Well, there are two. No matter how willing you are to sacrifice convenience for looks, prams can be as hard to handle as their passengers. Pushing one on a sunny Easter Sunday is great, but more often you'll be slipping out to the 7-Eleven on rainy mornings to pick up milk and it won't make you look or feel like Mary Poppins then. And then there's the cost. Three hundred dollars, on the low end might not sound like much to some of

Full hood

Real mattress

Tall handle

Foot covering

Spring suspension

Large basket

Removable basket can be used as a bassinet

Brake

you, but most babies outgrow a pram in three months. To me, there's no way to make that sound smart.

It Must Have

❑ Even if you can borrow a pram, **you must purchase a new mattress.** These are available in juvenile stores.

❑ There is no other storage area, so the pram must have a **basket** on the bottom.

You Might Want It To Have

❑ Some prams come with a **removable Moses basket,** which is a nice feature because it can double as a baby carrier or a bassinet.

If You're Borrowing

Most prams are handed down by family members. This is a nice tradition, but if you plan to push the pram that your mother used when you were a baby, drag it out of the basement *now.* You should let it air out for a while and get a new mattress—juvenile stores make mattresses for prams and they make hinged ones that allow you to sit the baby up as well as lay him flat. You will probably need spare parts, which are always difficult to find. You might want to measure the wheels, as some people find them at tag sales. There are places that renovate prams, but it will take some research to find one, so be sure to start the process now and not when you bring the baby home.

Your Budget

Prams are generally not low-budget items. In fact, the top of the line Silver Cross can cost you as much as $1,600 but they are not easily found in the United States. However, if you want the chrome look and springy feel without the price tag, you may want to look at the Inglesina Classic ($499 to $650 with an additional stroller seat for when baby is sitting up).

Perego makes a similar product line with smaller wheels and frame, but springy just the same. The Culla ($499) and the Arianna ($439) each have removable Moses baskets so you can use the carriage portion without the frame as a bassinet. You can buy a separate stand for this purpose.

The Kingston Plus ($399) also offers some of the comforts of a pram with the versatility of an added stroller piece and is somewhat smaller and less bulky than the others. It comes with an option of white or black tires in case the prospect of cleaning your white tires seems like one too many things for you to worry about. (Over time these white tires tend to turn yellow.)

Carriage/Stroller

- Must Have
- Birth to out of stroller (wishful thinking!)
- Great to borrow
- Price range: $100 to $399

Essentials
▶ Meets safety specifications laid out on p. 100
▶ Swiveling wheel sets
▶ Individual brakes for wheel
▶ Removable, washable seat cover
▶ Rain cover

AS I SAID before, the carriage/stroller, once considered the most practical choice in a stroller because of reversible handles that allow for use with the baby facing you as well as with the baby facing away, are becoming less popular as a result of a flood of new travel system products to the market. A travel system (covered in the car seat discussion in the Getting Around chapter) includes a stroller and infant car seat, enabling you to take the baby from the car and into the stroller without removing him. However, I still believe that the carriage stroller is the most practical choice for people in urban areas, who don't use cars every day, because the quality of the carriage/stroller is generally much higher than the stroller that comes with the travel system. It handles better and will accept more punishment with less wear and tear. All carriage strollers have reversible handles to convert from a carriage (with baby facing you) to a stroller (with baby facing away from you). They all have adjustable seats to allow the baby to lie flat or sit up. While the most important factors in this purchasing

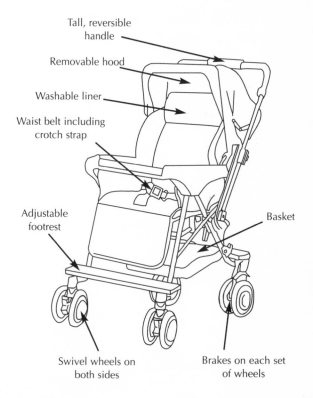

Tall, reversible handle

Removable hood

Washable liner

Waist belt including crotch strap

Adjustable footrest

Basket

Swivel wheels on both sides

Brakes on each set of wheels

decision are handle height, weight, and ease of folding, there are a few more fine points. It helps for you to consider whether you'll rely primarily on an umbrella stroller once the baby can sit up. If that's the case, you might want to borrow a carriage/stroller for the first few months and then spend more on the umbrella stroller. Another factor is your due date and where you live. If you're delivering in the fall or winter and you get a lot of snow and cold weather, you'll probably use the more heavyweight carriage/stroller not only for the increased protection but also for handling snowy streets and curbs.

Safety First

Carriages and strollers are one of the product categories for which the Juvenile Products Manufacturers Association (JPMA) provides certification tests. (As I mentioned in the chapter on regulation, it is not mandatory for a product to have this certification, and I recommend many products that don't.) This merely serves as an extra test of compliance with the Standard Consumer Safety Specification for Carriage/Strollers, the ASTM F833. The requirements are as follows:

- ❏ **No sharp edges or protrusions**
- ❏ **A locking device to prevent accidental folding**
- ❏ **Brakes that limit the rotation of braking wheels**
- ❏ **Load tests of the seat and foot rest**
- ❏ **Stability tests with child-size test dummies**
- ❏ **Stability tests which simulate a child climbing in**
- ❏ **Restraining system tests**
- ❏ **Specific labeling about not leaving the child unattended**
- ❏ **Labeling of certain key instructions**
- ❏ **Labeling with crucial manufacturer information and instructional literature**

I have a few more Must Haves of my own:

❏ There are eight wheels on a typical carriage/stroller—four sets of two paired wheels. Each wheel set must swivel. To save weight and cost, some carriage/strollers have only two swiveling wheel sets. This is not good; for optimal control, you must have the back wheels stationary and the front wheels swiveling. The cheaper models without four swiveling wheel sets are difficult to steer when they are in the carriage position.

❏ **Each wheel must have a brake**—not to stop short while you're going 50 miles per hour, like in a car, but just to prevent the stroller from rolling if you want to stop for any reason and happen to be on even a slight incline.

❏ A stroller must have **a removable, washable seat cushion liner.** Most come with a removable washable liner, but if yours doesn't, get one for $29 to keep the stroller cleaner (which is good if you're borrowing) and keep baby cooler in hot weather. A stroller liner must have the proper slots to run the stroller straps through. If you prefer, a cloth diaper or towel can serve the same purpose as a stroller liner. If you really want something luxurious, a lambskin liner keeps baby warm or cool and is very soft and cuddly. This costs around $69, but check first to see if baby is allergic.

❏ **A rain cover** for your stroller is a necessity. These are generic items, with one exception. Specially fitting raincovers can be purchased for the Maclaren strollers. These are good because they have a tighter seal that keeps baby drier. The customized MacClaren rain covers cost $21, and generic models are considerably less expensive.

❏ If you live in an area with cold winters, the stroller must come with **a boot, which is a flap that encloses the front of the stroller and keeps the baby warm.**

You Might Want It To Have

❏ Not necessarily a must, but a nice feature in some carriage/strollers is **a zip-off flap on the hood.** In warmer weather you can remove this flap, which leaves just a sun canopy, and the baby gets fresh air. Also, it's good for the hood to be on a ratchet so that it can be moved into any position to block the sun. The Peg Perego line offers this feature.

If You're Borrowing

You will only use the carriage/stroller for three to six months. After that you will want a lighter umbrella stroller. You should absolutely borrow a carriage/stroller if you can. You will be saving a lot of money that you can put toward a top-of-the-line umbrella stroller. If the stroller you are intending to borrow has wheels that roll, folds properly, and has an intact waist and crotch belt and functioning brakes, then you're in business.

Your Budget

I recommend the Peg Perego line of strollers. They have very good customer service, a one-year warranty, and spare parts that are easily obtained, and they come in a wide variety of fabrics. The shrinking market for carriage strollers is evidenced by the fact that the Pet Perego line now only contains two models of carriage strollers instead of the three offered in the past. The Milano-XL is the more expensive model, retailing for $359. However I have seen it on sale in discontinued colors from $250 to $280, so you might want to look around. The Venezia is the model I recommend because it is exactly the same as the Milano except the seat is three inches smaller and it is three pounds lighter than the Milano. They both offer adjustable handle heights, a large underneath storage basket, multi-position hood and foot covering for warmth and extra security (the straps are really what keeps the baby secure but the cover will make you feel better—always remember to use the straps).

A very inexpensive alternative to the carriage/stroller is the Graco LiteRider ($79). This is a simple stroller without a reversible handle, so you cannot face the baby, however the seat reclines far enough back for use with a newborn, it has a very large underneath storage basket and a high comfortable handle. It is quite bulky and heavy (21 pounds) but if you think you'd rather spend your money on the lightweight umbrella stroller this could be a good choice for you.

Umbrella Stroller

- **Must Have**
- Birth to 4 years
- Not good to borrow
- Price range: $29 to $210

Essentials
▶ Ability to fold easily
▶ Swiveling front wheels

AN UMBRELLA STROLLER is a lighter-weight stroller that reclines in anywhere from two to five positions. Most umbrella strollers have open handles that you can use to hang bags. But you must always be careful when removing the baby if you have packages on the handles because the stroller can tip backward.

It Must Have

❏ The umbrella stroller must be **easy to fold with one**

hand because you will often be holding the baby while folding it. You will be using the umbrella stroller for a long time and going from place to place (on and off buses and in and out of cabs, if you live in a city), so it had better not be a pain to fold.

❑ To make steering bearable, the front wheel sets of the umbrella stroller must swivel. Cheaper models do not have this feature; you have to pivot off the rear wheels to turn them.

You Might Want It to Have

❑ A nice feature is **a removable canopy** that blocks the sun and also supports a rain cover (although I've yet to see a two-year-old who will tolerate a rain cover.)

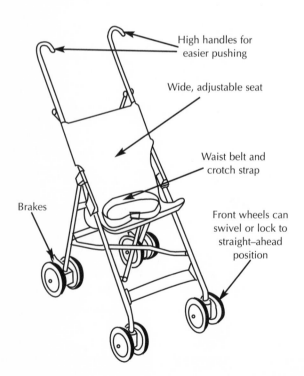

High handles for easier pushing

Wide, adjustable seat

Waist belt and crotch strap

Brakes

Front wheels can swivel or lock to straight–ahead position

Some umbrella strollers come with this; for the others, you must purchase the canopy separately.

Your Budget

The company with the best reputation and the most durable umbrella stroller products is Maclaren. All of these strollers have high, comfortable handles, wide seats for baby's comfort, are usually able to last until the baby is out of a stroller, and most important, feature simple one-handed folding. Choosing which umbrella stroller is best for you will depend on when you wish to begin using it, how many reclining options you want to give your baby, and how light you want it to be. I would like to state, once again, that it is important to purchase this product from a store with a very good service policy. The store should repair on-site when possible and offer a loaner if they have to send your stroller away. Find this out before you make a purchase.

If you would like to use an umbrella stroller with a newborn, you will need a model that reclines almost flat. This will make the stroller heavier. If you're reading this book, trying to save money on baby products, you probably wouldn't choose the Maclaren Titanium ($1999—yes. you read that correctly!) It has the same frame as the two products I will recommend next, but this frame is made out of Titanium, making it handy if you break your leg skiing and want to set the break yourself. The handmade seats are made from tanned leather. It just goes to show that in every product category there is always a product for someone with an unlimited budget. The Maclaren model I would recommend for use with a newborn is the Vogue ($199 to $249) or the Techno ($289). They both weigh 13.2 pounds, but the Techno has new ergonomically correct handles that are angled in. These handles may be more comfortable when pushing, but they make it harder to adjust the seat because you cannot get between the handles from the top of the stroller. You must bend down to adjust the seat backwards. Similar products that can be used with a newborn include the Perego Pliko ($199 to $249). The Pliko has more seat padding than the Maclaren and stands by itself when folded, however it weighs more (17.1 pounds). Another possibility is the Inglesina Easy ($229), weighing 16 pounds and offering a very nice selection of "funky" colors. Both the Pliko and the Easy have modifications for use with infant car seats.

If you are looking for an umbrella stroller for use with a baby three months or older, you will not need one with a fully reclining seat. Maclaren makes two models for this purpose. The Quest ($199), weighing 12.3 pounds, has three positions and a pullout leg rest for before the baby is tall enough for her feet to reach the footrest. If you're looking for a Maclaren that you'd start using at around six months, it's the Day Tripper ($169), weighing only 10.6 pounds. It has only two reclining positions.

For the more budget conscious, the CitiLite by Graco ($79.99) is a good choice. The CitiLite weighs 10.8 pounds, has a nice big basket, comfortable tall handle and folds very easily. The seat has no defined positions— you adjust it by pulling a strap.)

Jogging Stroller

- Totally Optional
- 4 months to 75 pounds
- Good to borrow
- Price range: $149 to $320

A JOGGING STROLLER is good for those of you who feel the need to run with your baby. This is basically a

> ▶ **TIP:** When you travel by plane, I recommend that you bring a stroller up to the boarding gate. If the flight attendants ask you to check it, ask to store it in the on-board closet. Checked strollers tend to get damaged en route. If you must check your stroller or carriage, you can protect it somewhat with the luggage-type bag made by Prince Lionhard ($29). It comes in carriage or stroller size. Since I do a lot of damage-claim assessments for the airlines, I would just warn you that this item can't save your stroller from being mangled by heavier pieces of luggage thrown on top of it in the cargo section. But if you do a lot of schlepping and need a bag with a handle, it's not bad.

three-wheeled stroller with big, mountainbike-style tires, so it's also handy for people who live in rural settings without sidewalks and smooth pathways. The jogging stroller does not provide the smoothest ride, so you should ask your pediatrician about the appropriate time to begin using one.

I recommend the Baby Jogger II, by the Baby Jogger Company. This is the most expensive of the jogging strollers but by far the best. Baby Jogger Co., formerly Racing Strollers, is a small company in Yakima, Washington, where the staff eats, sleeps, and breathes their products. If you have specific questions about the jogging strollers, give them a call. The aptly named Baby Jogger II ($310) has 20-inch mountain bike tires, a wide aluminum tubing frame, and wheels made of alloyed metal—they will not rust even if you are jogging on the beach. It also has a hand brake, an important feature that some competitive models do not include. Most of the competitors are also much heavier, not as steady, and have lower handles. The Baby Jogger II offers the highest handle, and an extra-tall size for an additional $50. For an additional $20 you can get a shock absorbing suspension.

This is a great product to get word-of-mouth advice on. You should ask someone who has one if she likes it. If you run, you probably see jogging strollers at the track or in the park. Maybe one of the owners will even let you try it. The store might let you do a test run around the block with one before you buy it.

Twin Carriage/Stroller

- Might Want
- Birth to Toddler
- Good to borrow
- Price range: $339 to $599

Essentials
▶ Each seat should recline independently

MORE AND MORE people have twins these days. You have several options for transporting them, none terribly attractive. (However, as the parent of twins, you will not be leaving the house much anyway for the first few months.) There are several products made especially for twins (such as a double-front carrier), but the twin stroller is the only one I'd consider.

Twin carriage/strollers are heavy, bulky, and rather costly. They are great to borrow; check out the local twins clubs for leads on borrowing or buying a used stroller. It is especially important to remember here that you, too, will probably need a lighter stroller when the twins are about three months old. So you might try to do without it completely.

Aside from purchasing a twin carriage/stroller, some people opt to use a large pram in which both babies can lie side by side. This is an option I recommended to my twin-bearing customers. Another alternative for solo strolls is purchasing a single carriage/stroller and wearing the other twin in a front carrier (while you simultane-ously spin a plate on your right index finger).

Your other option here is to use a twin umbrella stroller with fully reclining seats. If you're willing to sacrifice facing the babies in the beginning, this may enable you to avoid having to purchase two pieces of equipment. If you decide to use a twin stroller (espe-cially the wider side-by-side style), make sure to measure the doorways of your home, the elevator in your apartment building and even the doorways of stores you will visit frequently. If the stroller that you are considering will not fit your life, you will be very frustrated and you won't use it.

It Must Have

❏ The two seats of a twin carriage stroller **must recline independently** so that one baby can sit up while the other is laying flat.

If You're Borrowing

I wouldn't be too choosy here; however, make sure that it folds properly and has wheels that roll, functioning brakes, and safety belts.

Your Budget

If borrowing or purchasing used is not possible, there are two types of twin strollers available—a tandem-style carriage/stroller with one seat behind the other, or a side-by-side stroller with the two seats next to each other. In the tandem category, there are two prod-ucts that allow both babies to lie flat and allow you to face them. The major disadvantage is weight, bulk, and difficulty in folding. If you're in a rush, forget about it. It's at least a five-minute procedure: you must remove both seats from the chassis and then fold the chassis down.

The Peg Perego Duette ($359 to $499) has a chrome chassis with two separate removable seats that can be configured to face you, face each other, or face front. Both seats recline flat for newborns and feature removable washable liners. The carriage's spring suspension lets you rock agitated babies, and it features large wheels to support the weight. A full hood and boot can be purchased separately for around $150. The big drawback: bulk. Weighing over 30 pounds, it is nearly six feet long from handle to reclined seat. It is extremely difficult to maneuver through store aisles—or anywhere—because the wheels don't swivel. There is also no basket underneath, a minor omission compared to the other problems.

Another tandem carriage/stroller is the Inglesina Biposto ($429). For those of you expecting more than twins, the frame of this stroller can be adapted for use with as many as four seats. (In this case, the stroller could be renamed the "GoPostal.") The Biposto has the same features as the Duette and weighs about the same.

The side-by-side alternatives are a bit lighter, but their width can be a problem. And although the seats recline fully to allow the babies to lie flat, they don't adjust to face you.

If you want a side-by-side fully reclining stroller, look at the Maclaren Opus Duo ($429 to $449). This product has five reclining positions, weighs 27.3 pounds and is 29.3 inches wide. Another choice would be Maclaren Twin Traveler ($349 to $399), is slightly narrower than the Opus Duo and is four pounds lighter. There are lower-priced options from Graco with the DuoLite ($149 to $189) and the DuoRider ($129 to $169). The DuoLite weighs 18 pounds and is 29 inches wide. One feature on the DuoLite that could be considered a nuisance is one long front armbar that goes across both seats. This is not removable. It may make you feel more comfortable in the beginning, but it will eventually become a pain in the butt lifting your older kids over it. The DuoRider, weighing 24 pounds and measuring 30.5 inches, has two separate front armbars that are removable. You might find the Maclaren strollers a worthwhile investment even though they are a lot more expensive because they are narrower, fold up much smaller and are known for their durability.

> ▶ **SAFETY TIP:** When the baby is in the stroller you should always use the crotch strap and waist belt— even with newborns. Some people don't think they need to use the crotch strap with the boot, but it's a necessity. Accidents have been reported when only the waist belt was used and the baby slipped down and became entangled in the belt.

Accessories

Wool blanket/bunting—These items keep baby warm in the stroller. A wool blanket retails for around $40, and a bunting could range from $29 to $100.

Mosquito netting—If you are going to be in a buggy environment, this is a necessity, but in big cities it isn't. Many parents, however, like the mosquito netting because it gives a degree of protection from strangers who have a propensity to stick their faces inside the stroller to gawk at the baby. The price range on these is $4.99 for the basic netting to $21 for schmaltzy netting with ornamental bows.

Parasol—This is an umbrella that attaches to the stroller ($14 to $21) to block the sun. Older kids will pull and break this, so it will probably last only one season, but it does provide some added protection even if you already have a canopy.

Stroller toys—These serve no purpose until the baby can

sit up. Some toys require a stroller with a front bar to install the toy and others attach with a velcro strap. Remember that the stroller will be bulkier when folded with a toy.

Things To Make Parents' Lives Easier

Stroller cup-holder—This $6.99 device fits on the back of a carriage/stroller and has clips to hang bags on as well as the nifty cup holder (for coffee or a beer, depending on what type of day you're having). You can also purchase a drink-cup holder for an umbrella stroller for around $7.

Attach-a-bottle—This seemingly simple device is very useful. Basically, it is a piece of string that attaches to the top of a bottle at one end and snaps onto the stroller at the other end. No matter how many times Junior flings the bottle, it won't go anywhere. The same concept is available for toys called, you guessed it, Attach-a-toy. The bottle version retails for $3.99 and the toy model is $2.99. I once saw a mom use this as an "attach-a-bagel" for her teething baby.

Mesh bag—This is a $5 to $10 bag designed to hang on the stroller handle for easy access to key items. It's not great for storing loose change, but it is a good place to keep a spare bottle or toys.

Handle extenders—The concept is to raise the stroller handles to a more comfortable height. Not only do handle extenders not work well, the stroller cannot fold well with them. I do not recommend handle extenders and strongly suggest that you purchase a stroller with handles at a comfortable height for the main user.

After reading this chapter you may still feel uncertain about choosing your stroller. This is O.K. You don't need a stroller immediately after the birth of your baby. It is not something that needs to be ordered in advance, so don't panic about the stroller decision. Take time to ask your friends what they like and dislike about their strollers, consider your lifestyle, then make the call.

Getting Around

IN THE COURSE of a year, your baby will go from a little blob that can barely move to a dynamo that can get around your house faster than you can. During that time, you will spend countless hours dealing with, transporting yourself and your child from one place to another. On the other hand, you also will spend an equally enormous amount of time trying to prevent your child from getting from one place to another. I'm not sure, but this might be proof of some law of physics. Getting around is also not just about the baby; it's about letting you go places—to the bathroom, for example—by safely keeping the baby in one place.

So this section, too, gets around, suggesting different kinds of products—from diaper bags to swings—to aid all types of situations. All of these products can help you in some way to integrate the newest member of your family into your daily life.

Car Seats

The safest way to transport babies is in a child safety seat in the rear seat of your car. Every state has a child passenger protection law. Small children (usually up to age four) are required to ride in approved child safety seats or to use safety belts, regardless of whether they're in the front or back seat. Don't think that an adult can safely hold a child in a moving vehicle. Even a belted adult cannot protect a child during a collision.

You must have a car seat to take your baby home from the hospital. Molded from high-impact plastic, car seats are either freestanding or set in a stationary base, lined with cushioning and fabric, and equipped with a harness system to restrain your child in case you must stop short or you have an accident. Car seat requirements are federally mandated by the National Highway Traffic Safety Administration of the Department of Transportation, and therefore all the models you'll see in the store are deemed safe to use by the federal government. Your concern should be finding the car seat that works best for your family.

You should consider a few things before making a decision. The first is obvious: Do you have a car? If you live in a city and either don't have a car or rarely use one, you'll have different requirements from those of a family living in the suburbs whose car is a virtual second home. Factor in size, portability, and comfort, as well as your budget. If you're planning to use a car seat five times in six months, you might want to make less of an investment than someone who depends on it every day.

Second, do you want to buy both an infant car seat and an infant/toddler car seat, or just the latter? The pros and cons will follow in the descriptions of each product, but the general issues here revolve around budget and the amount of use the infant car seat will actually get. I consider the infant/toddler seat a Must Have and the infant seat a Might Want.

Third, do you want the newest model or something tried and true? Don't think too hard, because I already have an answer. In general, I recommend that you fight the temptation to be the first on your block to have the newest model car seat. Just as with new car models, there are usually car seat recalls the first year because lab testing doesn't tend to translate into real-world use. For example, a couple of years ago I got very enthusiastic about a new car seat that was inflatable. It was supposed to be great for traveling because it deflated into a little pouch and could be inflated in seconds for use on planes. As it turned out, the car seats deflated during use and couldn't withstand the pressure of airplane cabins. So much for that great idea. You may be a gadget freak who needs the latest and greatest, but car seats are not the place to feed your habit. Go with established products.

Finally, is it worth borrowing a car seat? Well, again depending on where you live and how much you intend to use it, there's a good argument for borrowing the infant car seat so the hospital will let your baby actually leave (though, given how fast mothers are shuffled out nowadays, it's hard to see them stopping you), and later buying an infant/toddler seat. And if a car seat of any sort is in good condition, is still in production, and hasn't been involved in an accident, it's always reasonable to weigh your options.

Read the next two sections, go look at the products, ask questions, and make the choice that will give you the most peace of mind.

Regardless of what type of car seat you choose, you should always consult the owner's manual for instructions and warnings. For example, some manufacturers recommend that you discontinue use of a car seat once it's been in an accident because the belts get weakened. Also, rear-facing car seats cannot be used in the front seat if the car has airbags. Certain types of seat belts (such as those mounted on doors) operate on an inertia principle whereby the belts only become taut on impact. These won't hold a car seat unless they are secured with locking attachments, which are metal buckles that deceive the inertia system into keeping the belt taut at all times and keeping the car seat properly in place. These items are all in the owner's manual, which you should read before use.

Also, infant car seats are designed to be installed facing the rear of the vehicle to provide the most protection for very young passengers. This helps to prevent whiplash if the car stops short. Infant car seats can only be installed this way, and infant/toddler car seats *should* be installed this way for the first six months. Many people have problems with the "facing back" installation, especially if bucket seats cause the car seat to pitch baby too far forward. To prevent this, you must create a level plane on the bucket seat before installing the car seat. This can be done with a rolled-up towel, a pillow, or a two-by-four. Your owner's manual will explain installation in detail.

Infant/Toddler Car Seat

- Must Have
- Birth to 40 pounds
- Okay to borrow
- Price range: $30 to $200

YOUR CHOICE OF an infant/toddler car seat will depend on how you intend to use it. If you mean to use the car seat from birth you will need different features than if you intend to begin after your baby is six months old.

Safety First

All car seats must meet certain federal standards in order to be offered on the market. A car seat cannot be used if it has been in an accident. It must be disposed of.

You Might Want It To Have

❏ **If you intend to use the car seat from birth,** the only suitable type of belting mechanism is the **five-point harness.** As the term suggests, there are five points at which the belt supports the baby—two over the shoulders, two across the hips, and one at the crotch. My reasons for recommending the five-point harness to parents who want to use the infant/toddler car seat from birth are twofold. First, other belts are too heavy for infants. The five-point

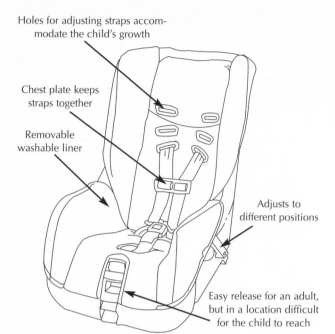

Holes for adjusting straps accommodate the child's growth

Chest plate keeps straps together

Removable washable liner

Adjusts to different positions

Easy release for an adult, but in a location difficult for the child to reach

harness provides the best support with the lightest pressure. Second, the other types of belting mechanisms, such as a front bar or a T-shield, are not only too heavy for an infant, but also (compounding your new-parent neuroses) obstruct your view of the baby, especially when the baby is facing backward for the first six months.

❑ The **fabric** on all car seats is **removable and washable**. Some models offer vinyl seat covers, which are easy to wipe clean; however, I strongly recommend against it. As you can imagine, in warm weather you will need a spatula to remove your baby from a vinyl car seat.

Your Budget

As I mentioned earlier, a budget-conscious car seat strategy is to purchase an infant/toddler seat and use it from birth to 40 pounds. If you do this, you have a choice of several seats with a five-point harness belting mechanism. The least expensive model is also the most popular. The Century 1000 STE retails for around $69, and I've seen it in big chains for as low as $49. Car insurance companies also offer discounts on car seats. The Century 1000 STE is lightweight, easy to transport, and has an adjustable seat incline. The seat is tall, with protruding wings to protect your baby's head. (The baby can rest his head on the wing to sleep.)

Evenflo makes a popular infant/toddler seat with a five-point harness called the Odyssey Comfort ($99). This features a nice cloth fabric and has a wider seat than the Century. Once the baby is sitting upright (after six months), you can adjust the seat position without disturbing the baby.

The Century Smart Move ($89) features the five-point harness as well as extra head padding and lumbar support (not necessary). What makes this seat different is that it moves on its base and is supposed to slide and deflect some of the impact in the event of a crash.

Another popular model is the Britax Roundabout ($200). As with other models, this seat can be used with babies weighing 5 to 40 pounds. The Roundabout was the first one to offer use in the rear facing position up until 30 pounds. The others up until recently were only able to be used rear facing until 20 pounds. Now many manufacturers have adjusted their products to accommodate rear-facing up to 30 pounds. However this will not be true of all models so check this out before you buy. It is recommended by the American Academy of Pediatrics that children ride in a rear facing car seat as long as possible to prevent a whiplash effect in the event of a crash. An additional safety feature of the Roundabout is very robust padding, similar to that used in bicycle helmets, under the upholstery of the seat. In other seats, ordinary foam is used. I consider the Britax Roundabout to be the best product in this category. It is the one I use for my own daughter.

I also want to mention a nice accessory product here called the Car Seat Buddy ($3.99). Sometimes car seat belts can dig into the baby's neck and shoulders, especially in summer months when very little clothing is worn. This product alleviates the problem by encasing the belt in soft fabric, which is fastened in place with Velcro.

If You're Borrowing

It's more likely that you'd borrow an infant car seat than an infant/toddler car seat. The former can only be used for the first six months or so—at which point most parents are very willing to get it not only out of the car but out of the house as well—whereas the other kind is anchored to the backseat for years. If you don't have a car or don't drive much, I think borrowing an infant seat makes a lot of sense. Be sure the borrowed car seat is in good shape and then make the investment in an infant/toddler seat.

You'll find a serial number and manufacture date on every car seat. If you borrow one, call the manufacturer to make sure that the seat was not affected by a product recall. Keep in mind that seats are often voluntarily recalled for minor flaws. If the model you are borrowing is still sold in stores, the government has deemed it safe to use.

I don't think I have to tell you to dust bust all the residual Cheerios and give the lining a good washing. And never use a car seat that's been involved in a crash. The belts can be faulty due to stress and the seat's plastic shell can be cracked, neither of which can be spotted easily.

Infant Car Seat

- Might Want
- Birth to 6 months (20 pounds and 27 inches)
- Good to borrow
- Price range: $39 to $120

THERE'S AN EXTRA plus in using an infant car seat: it can double as an infant carrier. Also, it's smaller than an infant/toddler car seat, and since a newborn is usually very small (we hope, for Mommy's sake), it seems to cradle the baby more securely than infant/toddler car seats do. You can use the infant car seat for approximately six months, but since its use is based on your child's weight and height (20 pounds and 27 inches), it might be added to the baby equipment junk pile in your garage after only four months if little Bob Jr. is on the beefy side. On the other hand, if your baby is smaller and still fits comfortably, I would continue use of the infant car seat past six months. The longer use you can get out of a product, the better, and the baby is safest in the car when facing backward.

Safety First

The same laws apply here as above, so don't worry.

You Might Want It To Have

❏ If you use a car regularly, **easy installation** is the most important feature of an infant car seat. You will not be very happy getting the baby in and out of the car if you have to constantly thread a seat belt through the car seat. It is also important for the infant car seat to come with a stationary base that the carrier/seat snaps into.

If Borrowing

Be sure to call the manufacturer to make sure that the product still meets today's safety standards explained, a rolled-up towel or cloth diaper serves the same function as a headrest.

The two most popular infant car seat brands are Graco (formerly Century) and Evenflo. Some of the models still carry the Century brand. In this category you first have to choose between a model with a base or one without a base. If you are using your car everyday and constantly taking the car seat in and out of the car for use as an infant carrier, or as part of your travel system, I would definitely recommend getting a model that comes with a base. The base stays fixed in the car, so there's no adjustment necessary once the base is installed. The newer

> ▶ **TIP:** When traveling on an airplane, some people opt to use a car seat. To do this, your car seat must be certified for use on an airplane. The flight attendant will look for the car seat's certification sticker. If you are going to a destination where you'll be using a car, you will most likely be bringing the car seat with you anyway, but it still might be easier to check it with your luggage.

models of infant car seats have adjustable bases to negate a possible steep angle that a bucket seat might create. If borrowing an older model, a towel or piece of foam would serve this purpose. Note, that when using a base, the handle must always be in the furthest back position, behind the baby's head, not upright, while in the base.

For those many two-car families, an additional base is available from $25 to $35 so you can use the car seat in either car without having to make any readjustments.

The only time you would purchase a non-base model is if you don't own a car because you will only be using the seat in other people's cars or cabs. In this case, having the bulky base serves no purpose and adds to the annoyance of having to adjust different car seat belts each time. I've also had customers who have brought a non-base infant car seat with them when going to foreign countries to adopt. It was easier than schlepping a base with them while traveling great distances.

Another choice you need to make in an infant car seat is in the belting system. Up until recently, the infant carrier/car seat was available only with a three-point belting mechanism. Now they are available with three or five point harnesses. It seems to me that in the first couple of months the five-point harness might be very difficult to use because the baby is often wrapped very tightly in blankets and buntings. The advantage of a five-point is that it covers the hips as well as the crotch and shoulders for an extra level of restraint. It could be difficult to locate the hips in very young babies. I would ask your pediatrician what he recommends here.

Evenflo's newest models are called Cozy Carry because of the newly-designed handle. Instead of having to click both sides simultaneously to make the handle move forward and back, you now push down with one hand in the center of the handle to move it. This is a simpler one-handed maneuver. You may also find the older model name, On My Way, on the shelves as well. The On My Way was the first Evenflo model to have en ergonomic z-shaped handle that is easy to carry alongside your body. The Evenflo products range in price from $69 to $99. Some of the newer models extend the lifespan of the product by being rated safe for babies weighing 22 pounds and measuring 29 inches, as opposed to 20 pounds and 27 inches. Make sure to read the product information especially if you already know that large babies run in your family.

The Graco product line is called SnugRide ($59 to $79). They offer products with three point harnesses that come with or without a base. The Century line includes various models with three-point or five-point harnesses, some accommodating babies up to 20 pounds and 27 inches and others for babies up to 22 pounds and 29 inches. One Century model name that you'll see often is the Vante. Century infant car seats range in price from $79 to $109.

You may think I'm being vague in my specific product descriptions in this area. The reason for this is that there is a lot of similarity amongst all of these products. They are all subject to the standards set forth by the National Highway Traffic Safety Administration. Therefore, it really depends upon your budget and taste. However, this is one product for which you should be sure to fill out your registration card and send it to the company. Recalls may occur at any time and you want to be assured to receive the most up-to-date information.

Car Seat/Stroller Travel Systems

- Might Want
- Birth to out of a stroller
- Good to borrow
- Price range: $129 to $299

A TRAVEL SYSTEM combines a stroller and car seat. As with anything, there are advantages and disadvantages to this strategy. In urban areas, travel systems don't seem to make that much sense. What the travel system is trying to do is enable you to purchase one item that will serve as both a way to transport your infant and your older baby with just the stroller alone. However, once your baby is too big for the car seat, you will never want to use the stroller that comes with the travel system because the stroller component is extremely large and bulky, cumbersome and difficult to fold (not to mention considerably heavier than your typical umbrella stroller). To try and get around the bulkiness, Peg Perego has designed its own travel system using the Pliko ($199) stroller and the Primo Viaggio car seat ($119) for one low price of $299. The only problem here is the car seat has already been recalled once for separating from the base. It is important to buy products like these with a track record. Stay away for now. If you are interested in one of these, the established manufacturers include Graco and Evenflo. You can often find travel systems on sale, especially if you are not picky about your fabric choices.

Having pointed out the disadvantages, people who are constantly in and out of their cars with sleeping infants find these travel systems a lifesaver. They enable you to transfer your infant from car to stroller without removing him from the car seat. If you think this might be important to you, the simplest and most economical solution is to purchase the Snap'n Go from Baby Trend

▶ PROTECTING YOUR UNBORN CHILD IN THE CAR:

Some pregnant women are afraid to wear a seat belt because they fear that the baby might be harmed by it in a crash. This is a fallacy. There is no evidence that seat belts increase the chance of injury to an unborn baby, the uterus, or placenta in a collision—no matter how severe. The main risk to an unborn baby is the injury or death of its mother. Mothers who wear seat belts reduce the risk to themselves in a crash, therefore reducing the danger to their unborn baby.

When wearing a seat belt during pregnancy, never place the belt over the abdomen. The lap belt or the lap portion of a lap/shoulder belt should be placed low, across the hips and over the upper thighs. The belt must lie snugly over the pelvis, one of the stronger bones of the body. Adjust the shoulder belt for a snug fit. If it cuts across your neck, reposition your car's seat for a better fit.

($39 to $59). This is a stroller frame that accommodates almost all infant car seats. Before selecting an infant car seat, you may want to call the company to see if your seat will fit. This is especially important when borrowing since this will serve the purpose of being a stroller for the first six months of your child's life, you may be able to skip the carriage stroller all together and go straight to an umbrella stroller.

Car Accessories

Secure View Mirror ($5.99)—When your baby is facing backward in an infant car seat, you might want this item, which attaches to the back window with a suction cup and allows you to see the baby through your rearview mirror. These are made by Children on the Go and Safety 1st.

Roll-down shades ($6.99)—If you've driven on the highway, you've undoubtedly seen these before. They are shades that attach to the window with suction cups, are see-through from the inside, but keep the sun out and off of the baby.

Car seat bib ($10.99)—This is one of the many examples of the seemingly limitless baby product industry. If you're one of the few people in the nineties who doesn't lease your car and you care what the interior will look like three years from now, you might want a rubber liner that goes under the car seat to prevent the upholstery from becoming matted, scratched or torn. Hint: a towel will do the job.

Neck Boppy ($10.99)—Who decided that if a baby's head droops forward that he is uncomfortable? The inventor of the neck Boppy. This horseshoe-shaped cushion keeps little Bert's head up in the car seat before he can do it on his own.

Baby Carriers

There are many options beyond strollers and carriages for getting your baby around, most of which involve carrying him somewhere on your person. And unless your person is your butler, it'll be your back and shoulders which will bear the brunt of the effort, so be sure you get the most comfortable product for you.

Front Carrier

- Must Have
- Birth to 25 pounds (or until chiropractic care becomes necessary)
- Good to borrow
- Price range: $25 to $70

YOU MAY THINK that once you've given birth your baby will no longer be attached to your body, but if those forty weeks weren't enough for you, don't despair. With a front carrier, Mommy's little "appendage" can remain comfortably intact for quite some time and Daddy can also experience the warmth of being one with baby, without the nausea and swollen ankles.

The carrier is a piece of fabric with two straps that cross diagonally behind the wearer's back, creating a front pouch for the baby. Sparing you the hassles of major equipment such as strollers or carriages and allowing you full mobility, the front carrier is the easiest way to get around. If you want to take a walk, you just strap it on, insert baby, and go wherever your heart pleases. This carrier can be especially useful if you live in an area with cold winters, where it's much easier to wear the baby than to wheel a stroller over snow and ice. There are indoor uses as well. Newborns like to feel your heartbeat, and the front carrier is the most convenient way to provide this comfort. When the baby won't sleep, many parents use the front carrier at home so that they can calm the baby while doing other things.

When making a decision about a front carrier, remember that your comfort is the most important factor. If you have back problems, see if you can try one out first, as any spinal stress will only increase as the baby grows. The bottom line is that if you're comfortable, the baby will be comfortable, and if you're both happy, you'll use it a lot. What's the point of getting one if you'll never use it?

You Might Want It To Have

❏ **The two straps that crisscross your back should be wide enough to support the baby's weight**. The straps should not have big, weird-shaped buckles that might dig in and be uncomfortable. For further support, a hip belt is a good feature.

❏ **When it comes to the fabric, less is more**. You may think that the baby must be fully enclosed to stay warm, but your body heat is often sufficient. When extra warmth is required, I recommend that parents wear the front carrier under a large jacket. I've also seen many people use a receiving blanket or cloth diaper wrapped around the front carrier to keep the baby warmer.

❏ You and the baby will be more comfortable if the baby is properly positioned within the carrier. **An adjustable seat** can ensure that the baby is positioned at the proper height on your chest. As she grows, the tush piece can be lowered, keeping her at a comfortable height on you. This also extends the useful life of the front carrier.

❏ Since a newborn has no neck control, the carrier should have **a high, pliable support for the back and sides of the baby's head**. Without this support, the head will droop to one side, which is not necessarily uncomfortable for the baby but could be uncomfortable for you if the baby's weight is shifted to one side. Also, you might find it more psychologically comfortable in these early days of parenting if your baby's neck doesn't appear as if it's bending in two. If your baby is small, adding a soft, padded insert like those used in car seats can also help give support and position. In addition to the head support, the front carrier should also have a solid back support for the baby.

❏ It is useful for the front carrier to be designed with **pockets** for bottles and other little necessities. Another useful feature is **a front bib** to protect your clothes in case of a spit-up incident in the frozen food aisle.

> ▶ **TIP:** Ideally, while riding in a front carrier, the baby's head should rest on the parent's midchest area. To get into that position, the baby should be installed higher, so that the head is above the parent's chin. The weight of the baby will then bring him down to the proper position.

If You're Borrowing

Since front carriers are worn high, they tend not to get as dirty as many other fabric products, and they can only be used until the baby weighs 25 pounds. Both factors make carriers good to borrow. Aside from the good cleaning you'd give it anyway, check that all the snaps and buckles are there and in good working order, and that there are no tears or rips, especially around the snaps.

Your Budget

For the budget-conscious, a good choice would be the Cozy Rider Soft Carrier by Infantino, at $19.99. This product has a high head support, very little fabric, criss-crossing shoulder straps, a removable vinyl bib and side clips for toys and pacifiers.

Another on the lower-priced end is the Snugli Out And About Soft Carrier ($29.99). This carrier features a one-shoulder design that is touted as being a better fit for adults with larger frames. However I have heard some complaints that this design causes shoulder, back and neck pain after prolonged use, especially as the baby gets heavier. If you go with this product, keep all the packaging in case you need to return it.

Two midpriced choices from a budget perspective are the Snugli Porte Bebe ($59.99), and the Snugli 3 Position Infant Carrier. The Porte Bebe is constructed of very little fabric (one choice is a navy faux suede) and features wide, padded, crisscrossing straps, a padded seat and a storage pocket. The 3 Position Carrier ($49.99) is described as growing with your child because it has adjustable seat heights and can be used with the baby facing in or out as well as on your back. It also features wide, padded, contoured straps, a padded waist belt for extra support and a padded backrest and head support.

The mother of all front carriers is the Baby Bjorn. For you aesthetically aware parents, the Baby Bjorn is a favorite because of seven fabric choices—there's navy blue, hunter green, wine, plaid, denim, light blue and yellow. Unfortunately, this variety comes at a price—$79 to $89—but this is the most comfortable and versatile front carrier. The Baby Bjorn features the least fabric (remember—this is a good thing), the widest crisscrossing shoulder belts, and a very pliable head support. There are also closures in front that adjust the carrier to four different positions. Front adjustability is a convenience, because Mommy and Daddy are not usually the same size and adjustments are constantly being made. And just when you thought there wasn't another good thing I could say about this product, there's one more: when baby gets a bit older and can support his head, flip down the head support and Junior can face out. This extends the life of the product because you won't mind using it longer if your baby can see things and can be stimulated. Junior will also stop spitting up on your chest.

Sling Carrier

- Might Want
- Birth to 25 pounds
- Good to borrow
- Price: $40

THE SLING IS the oldest form of baby carrier. It dates back to ancient China and Africa, where women working in the fields used slings to hold their babies. I think Moses' mother had the Nojo Babysling ($29 to $45). Operating the same way a sling for a broken arm does, the Nojo is basically just a piece of fabric that ties over the neck and spreads across the shoulder to support the baby like a hammock.

The NoJo Babysling is comfortably padded at all pressure points, especially the back and shoulder, and the deep hammock portion supports the baby with a strong but soft fabric that is machine washable. The Maya Wrap Baby Sling Carrier ($35 to $40) is another choice in this category. This product operates in a similar fashion to the NoJo, but it is made from hand-loomed 100% cotton Guatemalan fabrics. There are over 20 colors and patterns to choose from and the thin fabric makes the Maya Wrap less bulky than the NoJo. The Babysling was developed by Dr. William Sears, a noted pediatrician and author of many books on child rearing. According to him, the baby sling is not just a way to cart young Chloe around but a way of life. He advocates "attachment parenting," which he defines as "a lifestyle of getting close to your children both physically and emotionally." He feels that the Babysling is a crucial to this bonding process. Of course, we might have to wait 15 or 20 years to find out if kids that were held in the Babysling like their parents any better than we did. I'm not touting any child rearing philosophy here, but I've been told by many parents that not only is the sling a comfortable way to carry baby, but it is also great for breast-feeding. And the baby has a bit more freedom of movement in a sling than in a carrier, since her legs are not in holes and she is not held as tightly against the parent's body. But the biggest positive aspect of the sling can also be the biggest negative. The baby is very comfortable in it because she reclines in a very unconfined fashion. Since there's only a simple piece of fabric supporting the baby, some people are fearful that the baby will fall out. Obviously, this is an item that you should try before buying to see if you are comfortable with it.

The Carry-On Pull-Over Carrier by Leachco ($39 to $49) is a different variation of a baby sling. A loop of fabric with two armholes, the sling goes on like a shirt. It comes in cotton or fleece with plain or patterned edging. This might feel more secure to some parents than a traditional sling. Again, always try before you buy to see what's comfortable.

Backpack

- Totally Optional
- 20 to 60 pounds
- Good to borrow
- Price range: $49 to $199

Essentials
▶ Adjustable padded shoulder straps and hip support
▶ A sturdy stand-alone frame

BABY BACKPACKS ARE very similar to the one you might have worn when you tromped through Europe or the

Grand Canyon. All baby backpacks have a lightweight aluminum frame that allows them to stand on their own, usually with a bar that can be folded back against the pack once the whole thing is hoisted on the adult's shoulders. Within the frame, there's a fabric seat for baby and a strap so she can't leap out. The baby gets strapped into the fabric seat while the frame is standing open on the ground, then the grown-up crouches down and slips his arms into the big carrying straps, usually with some help. Most backpacks have outside carry pouches, so they are useful for walks that are too long for small children, and most fold flat, so they can be stored in the plane's overhead bin or in the car trunk. Backpacks don't provide much upper body support for the baby, so wait until she is able to hold her head up.

▶ **TEST-DRIVING FRONT CARRIERS, HIP CARRIERS, AND THE LIKE**

Don't feel embarrassed about asking to open a package to try these carriers. If the Gap lets you try on a pair of khakis or a blouse before you buy, your baby store should let you test these products, too—they're certainly no less expensive or important. Since carrying around a sack of flour seems a bit silly, ask a friend with a baby to come along that day—with the baby, of course—or if your friend has a carrier just try it at home.

The vast majority of people who buy front carriers give me good reports about their convenience, and, aside from the caveat about back pain, I recommend them whole-heartedly, but backpacks are a different story. While I've spoken with people who use their backpacks every day and love them, I've also heard horror stories of kicking, screaming babies pulling hair and vomiting down Daddy's neck. This does not sound pleasant to me, and, unlike with many other products, if your child does not like it, *you* will suffer directly. Remember that by the time Jason is big enough to be in the backpack, he's big enough to swat you on the head with force, bounce up and down violently, and perform such tasks as probing deeply into your ears. You should be prepared. This is a product that you really want to try out first with your own child. If you can't do a test run, try to borrow one. An even better idea is to ask for a backpack as a baby gift so you won't feel as though you wasted money if it doesn't work out.

All that said, backpacks can have their advantages. In urban areas with small store aisles and other difficult-to-wheel-a-stroller-through places, backpacks make it easier to get around with older babies, and they're just about the only way to navigate long walks on terrain more rugged than a city sidewalk.

It Must Have

A baby backpack needs to have:

❏ **Adjustable padded shoulder straps** for the wearer's comfort

❏ **Adjustable padded hip support** to transfer weight from shoulders to hips

❏ **A sturdy stand-alone frame**—Think about it. You can't take the baby out when she is on your back, so you have to take the pack off first. If the frame does not stand on its own, it will be very difficult to take the baby out.

You Might Want It to Have

❏ **A pouch** on the back is convenient for storage.

❏ While not a necessity, **a full body harness** to strap the baby into the backpack is available on some of the high-end products. The low-end ones have a waist belt to secure the baby, which would suffice.

If You're Borrowing

This is a great item to borrow. Unfortunately, up until the last few years, backpacks were made out of cloth (instead of the nylon they are now made from), so they were much more difficult to clean and more likely to rip. If someone is lending you a backpack and expecting it to be returned, don't borrow it. There's a good chance it will rip while you are using it and you definitely won't be able to return it clean. As with all carriers, make sure there are no tears in the fabric, the belting systems to keep baby secure still work, and the straps and waist belt are intact. Before you even attempt to borrow it, try it out with your baby to see if you really want it.

Your Budget

Lower priced backpack offerings include the Evenflo Trooper Backpack and the Compact Backpack by Baby Trend, both at around $50. These models both have lightweight steel frames and are adjustable for the height of the wearer. The Compact Backpack, when folded, fits into its own storage bag. The storage bag doubles as a diaper bag when back pack is in use and attaches to the frame. The Trooper comes with a roomy gear bag that snaps on and off. These products are not intended for long rugged hikes, just for light walking and shopping.

In the midrange, the popular choices are the Baby Trend Expedition ($59.99) and the Evenflo TrailTech Frame Carrier ($69.99). The Expedition features wheels that enable it to double as a mini-stroller, but you really wouldn't want to use it as a stroller because it only has two wheels, making it difficult to use, except on a very limited basis. This model also features a storage pocket that is difficult to get to. The TrailTech, on the other hand, is loaded with useful features.

Appropriate for babies 6 months to 45 pounds, the TrailTech features a fully padded seat with shoulder restraint straps and an adjustable, supported seat back. A fully adjustable, lightweight five-position frame ensures a comfortable fit for men and women 5 feet to 6 feet 2 inches tall. There is also an adjustable sternum strap for proper backpack positioning, variable load balancing, a large adjustable waist belt, and contoured, padded shoulder straps. This carrier also includes a toy loop, a removable teething cloth, a removable storage pack with baby bottle pockets, and a mesh back panel. The fabric is machine washable.

For the more serious hiker, the Evenflo Trailblazer Frame Carrier ($99) is a good choice. With a thickly padded waist belt, a lightweight plastic frame, and loads of size adjustments for parents and baby, the Trailblazer provides a safe and snug ride for baby once it has been adjusted properly. The carrier's child restraint system does a good job of keeping baby in the seat while you adjust the load-balancing straps easily accessible at the top of the carrier. To keep Mommy or Daddy comfortable, the carrier features contoured shoulder straps, waist belt, and lumbar support panel. The Trailblazer can be used for babies who are at least 6 months old and weigh less than 45 pounds, by adults who are between 5 feet and 6 feet 2 inches tall.

Another line for rugged use is Kelty, with products ranging from $99 to $199. These feature sunshades for baby and good waist and sternum belts for stability. Again, you must try these products with the baby inside to evaluate which model suits your needs.

Infant Seats

- **Must Have**
- **Birth to 9 months**
- **Good to borrow**
- **Price range: $29.99 to $99.99**

Essentials
▶ Secure straps
▶ A removable, washable liner

INFANT SEATS ARE the number three baby gift idea, behind mobiles and infant carriers. You will probably be inundated with infant seats, but at least they're useful, which is more than you can say about all the stuffed animals you probably have filling up the crib. Most customers I know like their infant seats very much; they don't require the room that a swing does, and if the baby is content hanging out in an infant seat, you may never need a swing.

Your two choices in infant seats are seats that rock— intended primarily as a way to quiet a newborn—and seats that bounce, which are meant be an activity for the little one. If you choose a rocking type, you'll have to do the rocking yourself by pushing the seat back and forth. The baby will not be able to gather enough momentum to do this on his own. A bouncer seat is formed by a piece of fabric stretched over a U-shaped wire frame. What's nice about bouncer seats is that they fold flat by coming

▶ **SAFETY TIP:** Bouncer seats should never be used on a table-top once independent bouncing begins—I've heard of babies bouncing themselves out of seats and onto the floor. Though all the stories I've heard had happy endings, why risk it? And while you're at it, always make sure the baby's securely fastened in the seat.

apart, so they are good travelers. You will have to start the bouncing in the beginning, but baby will be able to take over eventually when he puts on some weight—that's the activity part.

One way to save money is to use your infant car seat, which has a handle to transport the baby, and rock the baby in it. But since this is such a popular gift, you'll probably be more concerned with returning one than figuring out how to get one.

It Must Have

An infant seat must have:
❑ **Straps** to secure the baby
❑ **A removable washable liner**.

You Might Want It To Have

❑ A **bouncer** travels best, since it comes apart and can be stored flat.

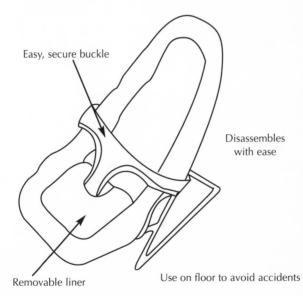

Easy, secure buckle

Disassembles with ease

Removable liner

Use on floor to avoid accidents

If You're Borrowing

This is a great item to borrow. If you are borrowing a bouncer, make sure all the rods (tubing) fit together securely. If your friends took it apart often, they might not fit as tightly as they did when it was new. In that case, you might want to tape the rods together as well. The main thing to check out are the belts and buckles. If these are in working order, take it and run.

> ▶ **TIP:** If you're borrowing an infant seat and the cushion is dirty, please don't buy an infant seat cover. These are generally $30 and up. If you call the manufacturer, you'll get one that's specifically designed to fit your adopted seat for half the price. If you say that you're using the infant seat for your second kid and you loved it, you might even get it for free.

Your Budget

There are many, many variations on this item. They range in price from $25 to $40 on the lower end and the manufacturers include Fisher-Price, Kids II and Evenflo. Some feature music or vibrating seats and there are many different diversions for baby—some in the front of the seat on a toy bar, and others on an arch that sits above the baby's head. There are higher-priced infant seats from Chicco ($70 to $80) that convert to toddler chairs. Again, I would be amazed if you don't receive one of these as a gift, but if you need to purchase one, just pick what you like and it will serve its purpose.

Swing

- • Might Want
- • Birth to 25 pounds
- • Good to borrow
- • Price range: $59 to $125

Essentials
▶ A wide base
▶ A removable, washable seat liner

A SWING IS for you—not the baby. Some people buy swings thinking that they're some sort of developmental necessity for the baby. But since you have enough to worry about, forget that. The glory of the swing is that if little Debbie cries a lot or won't let you put her down for a

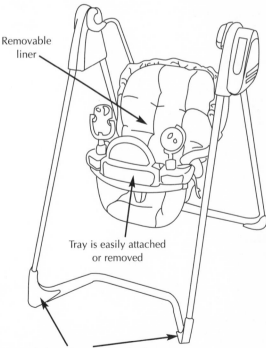

Removable liner

Tray is easily attached or removed

Sturdy legs sit evenly on the floor

second, there's a good chance that a session in the swing might afford you ten or fifteen minutes of quiet. This might not sound like a lot now, but it will allow you to eat dinner, take a shower, or straighten up the house—all wonderful activities that anyone who hasn't given birth yet should fully appreciate now while they have the chance. I credit my brother with dubbing the swing the "neglect-o-matic". If your baby is content staring at a black-and-white mobile and doesn't require constant holding, you don't need a swing. This will save you money, space, and the aggravation of assembling the thing.

If you've never seen one, a baby swing is nothing like you'd see in a playground, and you won't have to erect a jungle gym in your living room. You won't have to push the baby from behind or teach her how to pump her legs to get the thing moving either. A baby swing is motorized and consists of a molded plastic padded seat with a tray in the front that is suspended by two metal rods. The hanging seat is supported by a metal frame that is between three and four feet high.

It Must Have

❏ An **easy entry system**, which means the tray is hinged on one end to swing open, allows you to easily deposit the baby into the seat. You don't want to lift her up and over the tray. This is especially important if your swing has a motor on top, because then you have to negotiate getting baby over the tray without banging her head on the motor.

❏ A **safety belt** must be secured at all times to prevent the baby from falling out of the swing. Some swings have a solid plastic piece that goes in between the baby's legs for positioning. Don't mistake this for a restraint system. You must still use the waist belt.

❏ **A wide base** for stability

❏ **A removable washable seat liner**

If You're Borrowing

Borrowing a swing can be good but frustrating because your friend probably didn't save the instructions or might have misplaced some parts. I recommend borrowing this from an anal-retentive friend only. When borrowing a swing (as with any baby product), call the company to make sure the particular model was not subject to a recall. Before putting your baby in a borrowed swing, make sure that the metal frame and rods holding the seat are secure and cannot be pulled out without pressing a release button. Also, make sure that the frame feels sturdy on the floor and is not wobbling and, as always, check out the restraint system.

> ▶ **TIP:** Graco offers an incredible lifetime warranty on their swing motors to the original owner. Before you borrow a Graco swing, make sure the motor works—otherwise, have your friend exercise this benefit before you take it home.

Your Budget

You should stay away from a manual wind-up swing unless you are lucky enough to borrow one. Often the swing is the last bastion of hope for parents on the edge and if you must get up every eight to 12 minutes to wind it, your precious serenity will be interrupted to the point where it will hardly seem worth it. Plus, I've heard from some wind-up victims that after 10 minutes or so of swinging the baby will doze off or at least quiet down, and then the loud cranking upsets her again. However, Fisher-Price makes a winding model that lasts for 30 minutes. I recommend the Graco Six-Speed Swing ($79 to $119). The motor comes with a lifetime guarantee. It runs for over 100 hours on four D batteries. Also, the seat cushion is covered in classic navy fabric instead of a hideous pastel pattern that most models offer. The Graco Six-Speed has a wide base for stability, and the seat adjusts from almost a flat recline to upright. It also features a removable washable liner and six swinging speeds. (Thus the name.) The adjustable speeds are nice because, depending on the weight of your baby, you may need more or less oomph to get it moving. The Six-Speed also has four timer settings and four seat positions.

Graco also makes a Cradle Swing ($99 to $139) which enables a baby to lay totally flat and swing. Since I've never sold a swing to someone who intended to use it in lieu of a cradle, I don't see the necessity of this swing. The Graco Six-Speed reclines far enough for a baby to sleep and also allows the baby to sit up, so it is more practical. A cradle swing also takes up more room during use and storage.

Walkers

- Might Want
- When baby can sit up unassisted to walking
- Good to borrow
- Price range: $29.99 to $79.99

<u>Essentials</u>
▶ Brakes

YES, YOU'VE BEEN told by everyone not to use a walker, but the only person whose opinion counts is your pediatrician. A walker consists of a high-backed padded seat that the baby puts his legs through so that they touch the floor. The seat is supported by a frame on wheels. The seat height is adjustable so that most babies, no matter how tall or short, can touch the floor. However, some babies are just too small and then you have to wait to use the walker. With the walker's support, the baby can "walk around" or bounce up and down before he can walk on his own.

Like with many things, this device's problems tend to come from misuse rather than any flaw in construction. Walkers are not meant for extended use. Twenty minutes at a time is about all. There is some evidence that continued use beyond that can cause children to develop orthopedic problems. Walkers have wheels, so they can also be dangerous at the top of a staircase unless the stairs are gated off. The real question here, of course, is why the baby would be unattended in a walker near a staircase. Another problem with wheels is that they mobilize a toddler into a wrecking machine when it comes to your furniture and Austrian crystal figurine collection. The only kind of walker I would recommend is one with brakes on the wheels. Walkers have front trays, and some people find it easier to feed the baby in them at times because the baby is happy and occupied.

Safety First

The ASTM F977 Standard Consumer Safety Specification requires that an infant walker: have a locking device to prevent accidental folding; minimize the potential for scissoring, shearing, or pinching injuries; meet performance

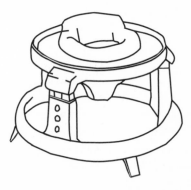

Exersaucer

requirements for tipping resistance and occupant seating area strength; have a warning label about leaving the child unattended, using near stairs, carrying walker with the child in it, and allowing use near ranges, radiators, and fireplaces; and have a label with the recommended height and weight of the child. Instructional literature must also be provided covering assembly, maintenance, cleaning, and use.

It Must Have

❏ A walker should have **brakes**. These don't stop the wheels from turning, but raise the wheels up off the floor so that the walker will remain stationary.

You Might Want It To Have

❏ A **toy gym that hangs in front of the baby** or a **toy that fits on the tray**, is removable and may occupy your baby when you don't want him to be scooting around.

If You're Borrowing

If you borrow a walker, make sure that the seat stays locked when placed in position at any height so that it won't collapse with baby in it.

Your Budget

A good choice for a regular walker with brakes is the Graco Tot Wheels 39—59 depending on the amount of toys ($49). This item features a removable activity gym to hang above the tray. If you are against walkers, there are products that will give your baby similar stimulation without the mobility risks. The most popular is the

Evenflo Megasaucer ($59). This is a saucer-shaped seat without wheels that allows baby to bounce up and down, to swivel 360 degrees, and to teeter back and forth (or it can be adjusted to be stationary). The Deluxe model, the Ultrasaucer, ($79) is exactly the same except for the sound-generating toys on the front tray. The negative is that this item takes up a ton of room. The Megasaucer is a great item to borrow from someone with a baby who is a year older than yours.

An interesting variation on the stationary walker is the Rotating Walker by Evenflo. I might want to wait twenty years to see psychological testing on the users of this product before purchasing one for my own child. This item consists of a stationary cylinder that sits on the floor that is attached to a little cart on wheels that the child sits in. The child can "walk" but instead of going anywhere, he just goes around the stationary cylinder in a circle, kind of like a dog chasing his tail. Again, I would await the research.

Jumpers

- Might Want
- When baby can hold head upright unassisted to walking
- Good to borrow
- Price range: $19.99 to $36.99

A JUMPER IS a baby seat attached to a spring that you hook onto a door molding to allow the baby to bounce around. You can adjust it so the baby's toes are just touching the floor. You raise it and readjust it as the baby gains weight and becomes more active.

It is better to use jumpers in wider doorways, since

there's the potential that a very active baby will bang into door knobs or a wall. For this reason, the instructions warn against letting baby swing in it. Before you purchase or borrow a jumper, you should discuss this activity with your pediatrician.

It Must Have

❏ For proper installation of a jumper, your wall must be at least three inches thick and no more than six inches thick. The doorway molding must be firmly attached and at least a half-inch wide.

> ▶ **TIP:** When you take a jumper home, don't destroy the box because it may go back to the store. There are a lot of requirements that your home must meet to make this workable.

If You're Borrowing

Before you borrow a jumper, call the manufacturer for a current set of instructions and be sure that you have all the parts. Don't try to install the unit with anything but the manufacturer's hardware. Check to make sure that all straps are secure and there is no damage to the seat, spring, or clamp. If the straps are frayed, do not use the jumper.

Your Budget

You can borrow a jumper, but since it is only $35 on the high side and there are a lot of precautions, you might just want to buy a new one. The jumper that I recommend is the Graco Jumpster ($30). It has a large tray in front but doesn't take up very much room. Graco also makes the

Bumper Jumper ($40) which features an even larger tray and a rubber bumper around the circumference of the seat that protects against banging up the door frame.

Portable Crib

- • Might Want
- • Birth to 18 months
- • Good to borrow
- • Price range: $89 to $149

<u>Essentials</u>
▶ Meets safety requirements for cribs [see p. 39]

WHEN YOU THINK of a portable crib you might picture an accordion-shaped, foreign orphanage–type of thing, but times have changed. If you need to cage your child

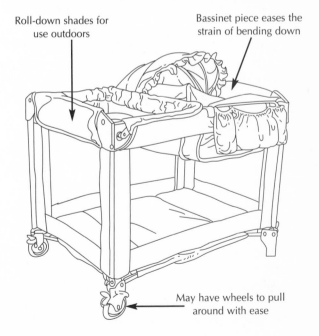

Roll-down shades for use outdoors

Bassinet piece eases the strain of bending down

May have wheels to pull around with ease

away from home, you have a lot more options than you once had.

The first thing you should know is that the earlier you begin to use a portacrib or playpen, the longer it will have a useful life. Once the baby begins to walk he won't want to be confined in this, or virtually any other, way.

The second thing you should know is that there are two entirely different products referred to as a "portacrib."

One product, which can truly be called a portable crib, is a small crib that can be moved from room to room. To qualify as one, the structure's dimensions must be 24 inches by 38 inches, meaning that it can fit through a standard door. A standard crib is wider than a standard door, so it has to stay in the room in which it was assembled (unless you have some insatiable desire to assemble and disassemble things with an Allen wrench). A portable crib is something you might want if the baby will be spending many nights at Grandma's house. The advantage is that it can be outfitted like a regular crib with a decent mattress. This also has its disadvantages, since it needs a bumper and the whole complement of sheet, rubber sheet and quilted pad layers that will need to be changed.

The other product, called a portacrib, is usually made with aluminum tubing, a thin, vinyl-covered mattress, and instead of slats the sides are made of nylon mesh. It is one piece that folds up into its own bag and can be thrown in the car trunk for a playpen at the beach or a place to sleep when the family spends the weekend at a friend's house. It's also fine to leave at Grandma's, as long as she doesn't mind this less formal rendition of a crib. This product is often referred to generically as a "Pack 'N Play", which is the name brand of the most popular of these items, the Graco Pack 'N Play.

Though you can certainly raise a normal, happy child without a portacrib, I think it's a Must Have if you have any intention of sleeping somewhere that's not equipped with a crib, or even if you want to just hang around in the backyard without worrying about little Otto making a snack of the begonias.

Safety First

❏ The safety requirements for wooden portable cribs are the same as those for full-size cribs. (see p. 39)
❏ Before putting the baby into the product, you should **make sure that all four sides are locked and the floor is taut and flat.**

You Might Want It To Have

❏ **A flip-down side** to assist in getting the baby in and out
❏ **Adjustable legs** so that it can be used at floor level as a playpen or a crib and takes up less space when folded. This is also good for older, more active babies because they can be closer to the floor if they do climb out of the crib.
❏ If you're using this outside, you may want it to have **mosquito netting** and roll-down **shades** on the outside to block the wind and sun.
❏ Some specialty shops offer an **additional three-inch mattress**, which is good to have if your baby will be sleeping in the Pack 'N Play often. It retails for between $30 and $40.
❏ Pack 'N Plays come equipped with one sheet. If the baby will be sleeping in it on a regular basis, you will need **extra sheets**. There are cotton/poly ($8.99) and all cotton ($12.99).

If You're Borrowing

A portable crib is a great item to borrow. But if you do, make sure that all the sides lock properly. And if your friends have used it at the beach, be sure to shake all the sand out of it, because this can affect the locking mechanism.

Before you borrow a portable crib, call the manufacturer and make sure that it is in compliance with all current safety regulations. I would also suggest getting a new mattress.

Your Budget

The wooden portable crib that I recommend is the Evenflo Foldaway Crib ($119 to $139, depending on the color). It has a flip-down side and adjustable legs. The crib is available in natural and harvest maple. It's also on wheels, so Grandma can easily move it around the house and keep little Otto in view at all times.

As I mentioned above, the Graco Pack 'N Play has become the Xerox of the portacrib market. It's lightweight nylon, folds up into itself and can be easily transported in the included nylon tote bag. It weighs 20 pounds and comes in two sizes. The smaller ($59 to $89) has interior dimensions of 26 inches by 38 inches and the larger ($99 to $139) measures 29 inches by 41 inches. I recommend the larger; the baby can sleep in it longer and it really doesn't weigh much more. The size difference just comes from more nylon mesh and hollow aluminum tubing. The Pack 'N Play comes in several color combinations.

Graco is the leading manufacturer of Pack 'n Play products that range in price from $59 for a basic model to $139 for the 5 Way Pack 'n Play that features a full-length bassinet plus changing station, which is an insert that raises a newborn baby higher so you don't have to reach down to the floor to get him in and out. This is a feature worth having if your newborn will often be sleeping away from home. After four or five months, you will take the bassinet attachment out because the baby will be too big and too active to be so close to the top. The 5 Way also includes a canopy, great for outdoor use, 2 locking wheels (not necessary) and a tote bag. Graco offers other models that include various subsets of the 5 Way's features.

Evenflo is another manufacturer in the portacrib arena, with their Play Crib ($75) and Roll & Go ($110) models. The Play Crib is a standard portable crib that very much resembles the Graco models. The Roll & Go is exactly the same crib but includes the bassinet insert as well as a cabana feature. The cabana is a piece of fabric which hangs about four inches like a canopy over the opening of the crib and serves as a sun shade so you don't have to schlep another umbrella along with everything else you need for three fun-filled hours at the beach. (It hardly seems worth going to the beach, does it?) The Roll & Go also has two wheels. Other manufacturers of portable cribs include Cosco, Baby Trend and Kolcraft, all offering variations on the same themes. Pack 'N Play manufacturers also make a "playpen" or "play yard" which is basically the same thing as a portable crib but is larger in size. The traditional playpen that we used to have when we were babies is a thing of the past. Most people prefer to use a Pack 'N Play, though since a playpen takes up a lot more room when folded and is way too cumbersome to take a playpen with you on overnight trips. If you want a playpen however, Graco makes a Tot Block Pack 'N Play ($99) that is 34" x 36" and features a cute bug design on each side.

Portacribs offer many different options and features. The ones that are important to you depend on when and how you'll be using them. If you plan to use it very often in the beginning, the bassinet feature is a plus. If it will stay at Grandma's house, a wooden one that is higher off the ground may make more sense. If you don't plan to use your portacrib outside, then obviously you don't need roll-down shades and a mosquito net. The choice is yours. There's no right or wrong decision.

You're just as well off buying a Pack 'N Play at a department store or chain store as you would be at a specialty store. You can often find these advertised in sale circulars for incredibly low prices, and you won't need any special training from experienced store help—just take it out of the box and set it up. If it takes more than five minutes, you've done something wrong.

Diaper Bag

- Must Have
- Birth to successful toilet training ($2\frac{1}{2}$ to 3 years)
- Not good to borrow
- Price range: $15 to $120

Essentials
▶ Portable waterproof pad
▶ Self-enclosed trash pouch

THE DIAPER BAG is your traveling changing table, refrigerator, toy chest, and—sorry to say—diaper pail. This is where you'll stuff nearly everything you need to keep Junior alive and happy when you take him anywhere from a stroll around the block to a flight across America. After about a week of trying to carry your purse at the same time, you will give up, and soon your wallet, your keys, your sunglasses, and whatever else you need to keep yourself alive and happy will end up next to the diapers and the A+D. Though you're hauling baby essentials inside, you're the person wearing the diaper bag, so this is one baby product you can afford to be selfish about. It's as much for you as it is for baby.

The smartest thing to do is to buy or find something that you'll feel comfortable using. You don't want to be stuffing stray diapers in coat pockets because you hate your diaper bag. Diaper bags range in style and price from $13 for a mint-green vinyl sack to $100 for the fake Fendi and Chanel. If you're casual—and "casual" takes on a whole new meaning once you have a baby—you might want to get creative and resurrect an old, favorite knapsack or roomy shoulder bag. If style matters and you feel you must have something new, buy a diaper bag. But remember this: No matter where you go, be it a fancy restaurant, a Fifth Avenue department store, or a mansion, people will still look at it and wonder if there's a doody diaper inside.

I don't recommend giving a diaper bag as a gift, unless you know the mom-to-be's taste so well that you'd feel comfortable buying her a purse. There are so many styles and possibilities that most people prefer picking one out themselves. Plus, Dad will probably have to tote it around some too, further complicating the taste issue. Diaper bags are not great to borrow. Three years of collecting Ritz cracker crumbs and having milk and apple juice spilled all over it should earn most diaper bags a long and happy retirement to the back of the original owner's closet.

It Must Have

There are no safety issues to be concerned about with the diaper bag, but there are two Must Have components:

- ❑ **A portable, waterproof tushy pad,** so the baby can be changed wherever you end up, be it the floor at the airport or your in-law's newly carpeted den.
- ❑ **A self-enclosed pouch** for any doody diapers that you can't immediately dispose of, or a soiled outfit.

You Might Want It To Have

- ❑ You'll be carrying your bag everywhere, so be sure it's

made of a **durable material**. Beware of vinyl covered with fabric; when you wash the bag, the vinyl will be ruined. Bags constructed entirely of vinyl, on the other hand, though not the most fashionable, are easy to wipe clean and maintain. Just be careful about leaving a vinyl bag out in the sun because whatever's in it will get hot and yucky, and I don't think I have to describe what that could mean. If you're going for a cloth bag, choose a fabric that has a bit of give so you don't tear the seams when you cram more and more paraphenalia into the bag. Popular, practical fabrics are nylons and synthetics, like raincoats or parachutes are made of, and also Thinsulate. Like vinyl, these materials wipe clean without having to toss the whole thing into the washing machine. My motto here is: Washable is good, but wipeable is better.

❏ **Pockets for bottles** are extremely helpful, especially if they are insulated to keep liquids cold or warm.

❏ **Clear pockets on the inside** help you get your hands on the wipes or baby powder quickly while trying to keep the baby from squirming off the tushy pad.

❏ The bag should have **several compartments** for clean diapers, a travel pack of baby wipes, a change of clothes, and a couple of toys to help Junior last another half hour in the car seat.

❏ **An adjustable strap** lets you either throw the bag over your shoulder or hang it on the back of the stroller.

To Buy, Or Not To Buy

Recycling an old handbag or knapsack makes a lot of sense—you liked it enough to use it before, so why not use it again? If you don't have anything to convert, you can just buy a bag that will probably be better-looking and less expensive than most ready-made diaper bags.

Buy a separate, fold-up changing pad ($5 to $10) and stick in a Ziploc bag and you'll have the two Must Have items taken care of.

Though I'm not big on ready-made diaper bags, they do have their advantages. A good diaper bag will come fully equipped with the features you want, meaning one less thing to worry about when you have more than enough to worry about. Also, given how much you're buying for the baby, it's a nice opportunity to treat yourself.

Keep a few other things in mind as you shop for a diaper bag. If you live in a city and use a Perego stroller, you may be tempted to buy a Perego diaper bag. Don't. These bags are expensive and small, and they tend to rip. While you might think no other kind of bag will fit your stroller properly, it's not true. You can buy generic holders and clips that will let you attach any bag to your stroller. One caution: Hanging a diaper bag on an umbrella stroller can cause it to tip as you remove your child from the stroller. You won't necessarily hurt Junior, but it will be extremely annoying.

If you'll be doing a lot of walking with the baby in a front carrier, you might consider a knapsack as the more ergonomic choice. You'll have better balance than with a shoulder bag, and your back, which will probably already be stiff, may suffer less.

Your Budget

There are so many choices in ready-made diaper bags—different fabrics, colors, and styles—that recommending specific brands here is not necessary. You can spend $149 on a fake Chanel bag or you can spend $14.99 on a vinyl bag with a Winnie The Pooh motif. The world of high fashion has gotten into the act as well with offerings from Kenneth Cole and Kate Spade.

Whatever range you go to, you'll get the basic features

you need. You might expect that an expensive bag would be in general more durable, with a heavy-duty zipper that is sewn in better, but in my experience this isn't often the case. The bag's durability depends on the durability of its materials. I say save the money and convert a tote or knapsack, no matter who you are.

Food

IF YOU'RE LOOKING for some answers from me about the best method to feed baby, you've come to the wrong man. You'll definitely get more than your share of advice, requested or otherwise; you'll read books and you'll probably talk to your pediatrician, too. You'll make a decision that best suits you and your lifestyle and you'll do your best to stick with it. My job is to help you get what you need to feed your baby and help him thrive in the first year, no matter whether you're breastfeeding or not.

When baby is about six months old, solid foods make an appearance.

This section addresses item by item the things you'll need in the first few months, before Oscar Jr. is eating solid food, with a separate discussion of what you'll need if you're breast-feeding. Then I'll go into the things everyone needs once solid foods start getting smeared around your child's face. And your walls. And your floors. And your furniture. And you.

Breast-feeding Equipment

Admittedly, breast-feeding knowledge is limited to the necessary equipment. If you have questions about breast-feeding itself, there are many books on the subject as well as organizations and lactation consultants you can contact. The market has swelled with a lot of paraphernalia that goes along with breast-feeding, despite the fact that this is a natural function that women have been performing since there have been mothers and babies. I'll start here with the items that will help you with the act of breast-feeding.

Nursing Pillow

- Might Want
- As long as you're breast-feeding
- OK to borrow
- Price range: $25.99 to $35.99

WHILE BREAST-FEEDING, it is important to keep baby at a correct height and angle against your body to encourage proper sucking and swallowing. One useful item to assist in positioning the baby without putting stress on your neck and arms is a nursing pillow. The pillow goes on your lap and the baby goes on top of the pillow, a comfy surface bringing her that much closer to your breast. Nursing pillows come in different shapes and sizes and there are really no Must Haves or Might Wants here, especially since the pillow that you just slept on (or that you're wishing you just slept on) will do the job nearly as well as any of these. Of course you can borrow one, too, but being a fabric item and given that both breast milk and formula not only stain but can remove varnish, you might want to start clean.

Your Budget

Again, there's no beating your own pillow for price and convenience. If you do want a dedicated nursing pillow, you have a few choices, all popular and all in the same price range. The Nojo Nursing Pillow, at $20 to $30, is on the lower-priced end. Viewed from above, this pillow looks like a bow tie, a shape that helps it conform to the mother's body. From the side view, you will observe that it is wedge-shaped to allow the baby to rest at the proper angle for breast-feeding. The Nojo has a removable washable terry liner, which you'll find very useful.

Another popular pillow that also wins the award for

Stupidest Product Name Ever is the My Brest Friend by Zenoff Products ($39 to $45). The MBF to us. This pillow is basically a giant belt that fastens around your waist with a Velcro strap. It looks somewhat like you're wearing an alphabet flannel–covered inner tube. The MBF provides a back support for mommy and a wide surface for the baby to rest on right at breast level while he feeds. The alphabet flannel covering is removable and washable and features a front pocket to hold odds and ends if you use it while traveling.

Probably the most versatile pillow is the Boppy ($19 to $29.99). There is also a Boppy 5 in 1 Fun with a removable play gym for around $49. The Boppy (now that's a good name) is shaped like a horseshoe, so it also wraps around the waist, but it doesn't fasten. Many parents also use it to prop up the baby before he can sit up on his own. The Boppy comes in lots of fun patterns and colors, but it does not have a removable liner so it is a bit trickier to keep clean. However they sell a Boppy slipcover for $10.99 that is removable and washable. If you're borrowing a Boppy this is certainly a worthwhile investment. Given the name and the packaging and the variety of fabrics, it's a fun gift to give, so the odds are good that you'll get one whether you want it or not. A relatively new product that competes with the Boppy is the Hugster ($25 to $40), a line of products in the same general shape as a Boppy but with a Velcro closure in the back.

Nursing Stool

- Might Want
- As long as you breast-feed
- Good to borrow
- Price range: $24.99 to $49.99

ANOTHER ITEM THAT helps position you and the baby comfortably for breast-feeding is a nursing stool. It elevates your feet to put your body at a comfortable angle and, like the nursing pillow, it brings you and baby closer without straining. It can be used with or without a nursing pillow, depending on the sizes of bodies involved and their postures. Note that I've listed pillows and stools as Might Wants because there's no guarantee that you'll ever need them or want them. On the other hand, they are commonly used by breast-feeding mothers. If you're having difficulty breast-feeding and you're not using either of these, your lactation counselor will probably recommend them as possible ways to ease the process.

Like the nursing pillow, there are no real Must Haves or Might Wants with a nursing stool, and you can surely find a substitute around the house if you don't want to spend the money. Let's face it, for thousands of years mothers have been making do without specially designed nursing stools. Of course, they made do without penicillin, too, so what do I know? Still, an ottoman, toy chest, or stool can serve this duty. The one thing that most nursing stools have that regular stools don't is a slight angle that slopes downwards towards you. The best solution of all is to borrow one. Made of wood, nursing stools are essentially little pieces of furniture with no moving parts to break, so they last a long time.

Your Budget

To avoid spending any money on a stool at all, you could probably find something in your house that will serve the purpose of elevating your feet to better align your posture for more comfortable breast-feeding—a wastepaper basket turned upside down, the cardboard diaper carton, your coffee table, or a lethargic German Shepherd. If you are interested in purchasing one, the basic wooden nursing stool generally retails in the $30

range. Rumble Tuff and Medela are the two main manufacturers. Both are solid wood and are "scientifically
engineered" to achieve proper angle to reduce stress on
your legs, back, shoulders, and arms.

Breast Pump

- Might Want
- As long as you breast-feed
- Bad to borrow
- Price range: $24.99 to $269
- Rental: $1.50 per day

Essentials
▶ Adjustable suction
▶ Portable

WHEN YOU BEGIN breast-feeding your newborn, you will
be nursing about every two hours. After a few weeks, it
is very possible that you'll want someone else to share in
the fun of feeding. If you are a working mother and want
to continue breast-feeding, the only way of providing
breast milk when someone else feeds your baby is to
pump your milk. Pumping is also sometimes necessary
to prevent the breasts from becoming engorged, a condition that sometimes occurs when the baby does not
remove enough milk from the breasts and they become
hard and painful.

A breast pump consists of a funnel-shaped plastic
cup (or two, if it is designed to pump both breasts
simultaneously—this is called "double-pumping").
The wide opening is placed over the breast and funnels
into two pathways—one that leads to an empty bottle,
and one that leads to the suction mechanism. If the
breast pump is electric, the suction mechanism is a
tube connected to a motor. If it's manual, the mechanism

is a cylindrical plunger that looks like a large syringe. When the suction begins, the milk is extracted from the breast and routed into the empty bottle. Don't worry, although some women say that they feel like cows during the pumping procedure, breast pumps are not complicated or frightening. Once you get the hang of it, you will find pumping to be an indispensable convenience.

It Must Have

❑ The breast pump you use must have **adjustable suction**. Every woman is different and if the breast pump is not comfortable, you will not use it.

❑ **It should be portable**. If you're purchasing an electric breast pump, it should work on batteries as well as an AC adapter so that it is completely portable. Keep in mind that when a breast pump runs on batteries the suction will not be as powerful. I do not recommend the battery-powered breast pumps for this reason.

You Might Want It To Have

❑ **Double-pumping capability**: If you will be pumping at work, where your time is limited, you might want to pump both breasts simultaneously.

Manual Versus Electric

There are both manual and electric breast pumps; your choice really depends on your lifestyle. The electric breast pump creates suction via a motor, and the manual pump uses a cylindrical plunger that the mother must pump to create suction. If you will be staying home and won't need to pump very often, a manual pump is a good choice. An electric pump is twice as fast as a

Double breast pump

manual one, so if you are pressed for time (like on your lunch break at work) it might suit you better. If you use an electric pump that allows for double-pumping, it is four times as fast. With this type, you can complete a pumping session in 15 minutes, as opposed to an hour with a manual one-breast-at-a-time model. However, manual pumps are smaller and lighter (under one pound, as opposed to five to seven pounds for an electric). A manual pump also gives you more control over the suction, which some people find more comfortable. From what mothers tell me, the suction of electric pumps can sometimes be irritating, but there's a new generation of electric pumps with built-in mechanisms that supposedly protect sensitive skin against excessive or prolonged suction.

Your Budget

Before you leave the hospital, ask to try the Medela Lactina Plus. This pump has a strong motor and allows you to pump both breasts at once, the quickest procedure. This pump is usually rented rather than purchased at a cost of around $1.50 per day (this is usually on a sliding scale—the longer you rent, the cheaper it becomes). I recommend renting an electric pump like this larger double unit, especially if you will be breast-feeding for a long time. The motors on smaller electric models don't hold up for very long or allow for double-pumping. If you were to purchase the Medela Lactina Plus it would be over $500, so renting is cost effective. To find a rental location in your area visit www.medela.com or call 1-800-435-8316.

One hidden cost of renting a breast pump is replacing the attachment that goes from you to the motor. Obviously, for sanitary reasons you want the pieces that touch your body to be new. The single kit sells for $26 to $35, and the double-pumping, or universal kit, sells for $35 to $50.

If you're still interested in purchasing an electric breast-pump, I recommend the Medela Pump In Style ($269) as a good double pump option. This product comes with several choices in carrying cases—shoulder options as well as a backpack. For a single pump, I recommend either the Gerber ($49 to $69) or the Medela Mini Electric ($69 to $85). The obvious benefit of the Gerber is that it is less expensive, but I've gotten better feedback from users of the Medela. This is the product my wife used and she was very pleased with it. The Medela can be operated manually, by battery, or by motor, and has adjustable pumping speeds. If purchasing a Medela pump, make sure to purchase extra membranes—these little (easily lost) white plastic disks create the suction. Without these, the pump is useless. The Gerber, however, has an unconditional money-back guarantee to mail back with the receipt, so you might want to try it and see if you like it.

If you only need to express milk occasionally, a manual breast pump may be the way to go. Manufacturers of manual pumps include Gerber, Avent, Medela and Evenflo, with prices ranging from $20 to $50.

The other odds and ends you will need if you're breast-feeding include nursing pads and breast shields. You might also want breast cream, but you should talk to your lactation counselor, pediatrician, or gynecologist about those.

To store breast milk, you have several options. You can express milk directly into a bottle and keep it in the refrigerator for up to 72 hours. If you would like to freeze your breast milk, you can also use a bottle, but most of my customers prefer to use plastic bags because they don't take up as much room in the freezer. Medela makes bags that fit directly on the breast pump, but these are very expensive—$20 for 50. What many people do instead is to buy the plastic bags from the Playtex disposable bottle system, which are $4 for 100. This requires that you transfer milk from a bottle to the bags, but it certainly is less expensive.

Nursing Pads

- Must Have
- As long as you breast-feed
- Bad to borrow
- Price: $6.99 for 4 reusable $6.99 for 60 disposable

NURSING PADS TUCK inside your bra to prevent milk from leaking through your shirt. They come in disposable or washable models. The most popular disposable nursing pads are from Gerber. I've heard from many customers that they are lined better and do not leak. On the other hand, some mothers report that the washable ones breathe more and allow more air circulation. The arguments against disposable and for washable come down to sensitivity, cost and environment—you'll have to decide.

Breast Shields

- Might Want
- As long as you breast-feed
- Bad to borrow
- Price: $7.99 for pack of 2

BREAST SHIELDS ARE circular plastic guards that help prevent nipple soreness. They are plastic circles with holes in the center. The nipple sticks out of the center hole and offers some protection while allowing the baby to suck. They're also used at times when you're not breast-feeding to prevent sensitive nipples from coming into contact with anything irritating. You will be fine with a pack of two. They're made by both Avent and Medela.

Bottles and Nipples

- Must Have
- Birth to longer than you think
- Not good to borrow
- Price range: $1.49 to $4.99

IF YOU'RE PLANNING on only breast-feeding and you're staying at home, good luck and feel free to move on to the next section. If you're breast-feeding but you're also expressing, this section is for you as well as for the formula people.

Among all the other things to fret about, even choosing bottles and nipples can frustrate parents—mostly because it's not wholly up to you which kind you'll wind up using. There are four major manufacturers of bottle systems, all of which I'll describe, but even if you make a well-considered decision and buy all the paraphernalia, there's a good chance that Baby Uma won't like the type you selected. She'll reject the nipple, scream, and cry, and you'll get nervous because she's not eating enough.

So here's the first tip: Buy one of each kind of bottle and nipple that you're considering and let the baby make the call. You'll save time, money, and ulcer medicine—and I promise that you won't spoil the baby.

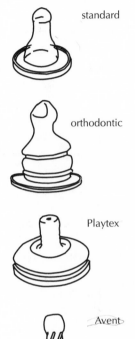

standard

orthodontic

Playtex

Avent

To bottle-feed, the main choices are disposable versus non disposable, glass versus plastic, standard nipples versus orthodontic ones, and latex rubber nipples versus silicone. As I said before, the type of nipple your baby likes is the most important factor in determining the bottle-feeding system you end up with, so you'll have to experiment a bit at the beginning.

The most popular nondisposable bottle systems are made by Evenflo, Gerber, Johnson & Johnson (Healthflow), and Avent. Evenflo is the only company that offers a choice of plastic or glass bottles. All of the others are plastic. There are some people who are convinced that glass is the only material that can get truly clean, but since all the others are made of plastic that can withstand sterilization temperatures, I don't know if this theory has any merit. Glass is certainly a bigger pain.

The theory behind Johnson & Johnson's Healthflow is

that the angled bottle will reduce the baby's intake of air and gas if the parent holds it properly. I feel that the four-ounce size for a newborn is a waste because you still have to hold the bottle up—the baby can't hold the bottle on his own—and it must be held in one position. Also, the angled bottle takes up more room in your diaper bag as well as in the dishwasher.

With Evenflo, Gerber, and Healthflow bottles you can use any kind of nipple. Your choices are between shapes—standard or orthodontic—and materials—rubber or silicone. Standard nipples are probably what you picture when you think of a bottle nipple—wider on the bottom, tapering off to a narrower, rounded tip. Orthodontic nipples, recommended by some doctors, are flatter and wider—more like a mother's nipple. Silicone nipples are becoming popular now because they don't get as sticky as rubber nipples. Also, rubber nipples become enlarged and cracked after two to three months and must be replaced. Although they supposedly last longer, silicone nipples are harder than rubber, and your baby might not like them.

Manufacturers of nipples that can be used on the nondisposable Gerber, Evenflo, or Healthflow bottles include Gerber (they make Nuk, which is an orthodontic nipple, and the Gerber standard nipple); Evenflo (a wide variety of color-coded nipples with different size openings for different fluids); and Pur (only silicone nipples). Once again, your baby will express a preference, and you will follow it.

Avent is an English manufacturer of bottle systems. This system requires that you use the Avent nipple, so if your baby doesn't like it you won't be using it. Avent claims that their system is "medically proven to reduce colic in the newborn" because of a patented nipple that reduces air intake while feeding. Avent professes that since this nipple is closest to the natural human shape and allows the baby to "suckle" (a long, slow, continuous lick that babies sometimes do on the breast) as well as suck, this is the best system to alternate with breast-feeding. All this is well and good, but only if your baby likes the nipple.

Disposable bottle systems are available from Playtex, Avent and Evenflo. A disposable bottle basically consists of a plastic bag that gets filled with milk and is contained within the hard plastic shell, or holder. These systems also come with their own nipples, but adapters are available that allow you to use other nipples. I've been told by many parents that the adapters are very annoying because they leak, so if your baby doesn't like the nipples that come with these systems you might not want to use them. Playtex and Evenflo also tout their systems as the closest to breast-feeding and as the best to use if you're alternating with breast-feeding. They both claim that their system can reduce air intake (and therefore baby discomfort) because of patented technology.

The biggest plus to disposable systems is that you don't have to sterilize bottles. You simply use a fresh plastic liner for each bottle. Disposable bottles do take more time to fill—there is a whole procedure: the plastic liner must be inserted into a holder, wrapped around the lip of the holder, pulled on the bottom to remove wrinkles, filled, secured with a ring, etc., etc. And if your environmentally conscious friend comes over, you might want to hide your disposable bottles because they do contribute a great share of non-biodegradable plastic to the earth.

Regardless of what bottle systems you decide to try, I recommend having an initial supply of around six four-ounce bottles. If you are breast-feeding, you may need even fewer (because you only need bottles for expressed milk). Don't get the eight-ounce bottles in the beginning; a newborn will never eat that much, and if you're pumping breast milk you will be frustrated at your inability to fill an eight-ounce bottle. Resist the urge to buy decorated bottles because they cost around three times more than plain ones (and they're not three times as cute).

Expect to purchase several types of nipples and experiment to determine which type your baby adapts to best. You will start with newborn-size nipples and eventually move to a three- to six-month nipple. The difference in these nipples is the size of the opening—a bigger opening allows the baby to get more food.

Always purchase extra bottle hoods and disks because they tend to get lost. These parts are interchangable between the nondisposable Evenflo and Gerber bottle systems. For the others, you must stick to your brand. You will also need a bottle and nipple brush for cleaning. I recommend that you purchase two separate brushes rather than to a two-headed brush for bottles and nipples. The individual ones have handles that are easier to grip for better leverage. I recommend buying a dishwasher cage ($8.00) which is a little enclosed plastic cage to keep nipples, caps, rings and disks from getting lost in the dishwasher. Note: many pediatricians say that the dishwasher water is hot enough to suffice as sterilization. You should discuss this with your pediatrician. A bottle rack ($11.99) is another useful item. It's basically a rack with sticks coming out of it to dry and store bottles.

Avent makes a bottle warmer ($39) that has a thermostat, a neat feature that lets you warm even a disposable bottle without cooking it. There is a cheaper version made by Gerber ($12.99), but you must watch it closely, since it gets hot very quickly and can burn your milk or formula.

Sterilization

If you are unfortunate enough not to own a dishwasher, or if you do own one but still want to sterilize your bottles, there are several methods of doing this. You can sterilize them on top of your stove in a pot and buy a

Safety, it is not mandatory for a product to have this certification, and I recommend many products that don't. This merely serves as an extra test of compliance with the Standard Consumer Safety Specification for High Chairs, called the ASTM F404. The major requirements include:

- ❏ **No sharp edges or protrusions**
- ❏ **Minimum withdrawal force for caps and plugs that a child can grasp between thumb and forefinger**
- ❏ **Drop tests of tray**
- ❏ **Disengagement tests of tray**
- ❏ **Load and stability tests of chair**
- ❏ **Protection from coil springs and scissoring**
- ❏ **Maximum size of holes**
- ❏ **Restraining system tests using a test dummy**
- ❏ **Labeling about never leaving child unattended and manufacturer labeling**
- ❏ **Instructional literature.**

You Might Want It To Have

- ❏ **A very large food tray** will result in less food on the floor, which is a good thing.
- ❏ **The tray should slide in and out and be removable with one hand.** Because your hands will be at a premium, it is important that a chair be operable with one hand.
- ❏ **A wide base** on the chair for stability.
- ❏ **A removable, washable seat liner**, since the high chair is a danger zone for messes.
- ❏ **A passive restraint.** All new highchairs now have a hard plastic bar between the baby's legs as a safety feature.

If You're Borrowing

If you decide to borrow a high chair, the most important things to make sure of are that the restraint system is intact and that the tray operates properly. Examine the back piece and tush cushion, and if they look worn you should call the manufacturer's 800-number and request replacements. If there is no instruction manual, you should request one of those as well.

Your Budget

Wooden high chairs are the most aesthetically attractive choice, but functionally they leave much to be desired. They range in price from $120 to $259, and there are some even higher-priced designer models, about which I can only say they must have been designed by people who don't have kids. To me, a wooden high chair is a big mistake for many reasons. First, the baby is less comfortable in a wooden high chair because the seat is not cushioned. To make the baby comfortable, you must insert a washable cloth liner, but it gets so disgusting that you will probably end up purchasing three of them (at $30 a pop) during the baby's reign in the high chair. The tray on a wooden high chair can not be operated with one hand and the sliding mechanism is metal on metal, which is neither smooth nor easy. A wooden high chair doesn't fold, so it must be disassembled for storage, and if you're like me, you'll definitely lose the screws before dragging it out again for a second child. On the other hand, millions of children have eaten millions of meals in wooden high chairs without it killing them, so if you simply can't co-exist with a plastic one, I recommend a simple Rochelle wooden high chair ($139 to $149).

In theory, wheels give high chairs mobility. Urban dwellers, beware: just because it sounds convenient doesn't mean that it's convenient for you. In reality, wheeled chairs are so bulky that you won't have much room to roll them around in. High chairs on wheels only make sense for homeowners who have a lot of different places where they might feed the baby, such as the patio, dining room, and kitchen, and all three rooms are big enough to handle a high chair comfortably.

A very popular high chair on wheels is the Prima Pappa by Peg Perego ($169 to $179). This chair features a large tray that can be operated with one hand, and is offered with a choice of several cloth or vinyl fabrics. On some models, they also offer a nice feature called a "dinner tray" which is a double tray. The top one comes off so it can be washed easily. I would go with the vinyl for an item that will constantly be covered with food. The Prima Pappa also folds flat for storage. The Prima Pappa Roller ($199) has the same high chair and tray as the regular Prima Pappa but this model has a handle and carry basket on the back for maximum mobility. It doesn't fold and it takes up a ton of room. Peg Perego describes this product as an eat sleep center because the chair can be reclined with one hand to 7 height and 4 recline positions. I don't see the value of this because there are plenty of other places that baby will sleep. He doesn't have to sleep in his high chair.

Another model on wheels is the Evenflo Easy Comfort ($99 to $109). This chair folds easily and features adjustable heights and reclining positions. I would not recommend this chair however because the tray sits too far away from the baby and therefore lots of food will fall off onto the seat. Additionally, this chair has vinyl fabric that is topped with cloth that defeats the whole purpose of it being wipeable.

A good choice for the budget-conscious is the Graco Easy Seat ($39.99 to $59.99). This chair features adjustable heights, a big tray with easy one-hand operation and a removable seat for easy cleaning. Although it doesn't fold, the seat does not have a very wide footprint.

Booster Seat

- Might Want
- 6 months to 2 years
- Good to borrow
- Price range: $29 to $40

Essentials
▶ Three supporting straps
▶ Wider in the seat and taller in the back

A BOOSTER SEAT attaches to a chair and is used for feeding baby while traveling, in restaurants, at grandparents' homes, or to replace a high chair in your own home if space is limited. When you think of a booster seat, you might think of the molded plastic boxes found in restaurants that are only one step above using a telephone book to raise a toddler to a more comfortable level at the table. The booster seat that I want you to consider is for a six-month-old and is more of a high chair without legs. It comes with a restraint system and a removable front tray. Any high-backed chair can hold baby and booster seat comfortably; just don't pick a chair that's valuable or an heirloom—it will get very dirty. You'll secure the booster seat to its designated chair by two straps; one circling the chairback, and the other going around the seat.

It Must Have

❏ A booster seat must have **three supporting straps**— one around the back of the chair, one around the seat of the chair, and one to secure the baby.

❏ You'll be sorry if you don't have a **dedicated chair** to use with the booster seat. This chair should be one that you don't care about, because it will take a beating.

❏ For added stability, make sure that the chair you are

using the booster seat with is **wider in the seat and taller in the back** than the booster seat is.

If You're Borrowing

It is very important to check a booster seat's straps. If you are borrowing a booster seat, make sure that the straps are intact and all buckles are working properly, because replacement straps are not easy to find.

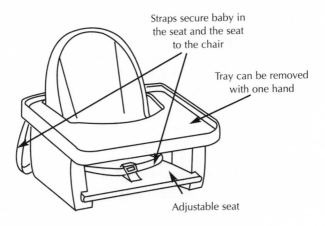

Straps secure baby in the seat and the seat to the chair

Tray can be removed with one hand

Adjustable seat

Your Budget

The only booster seat I will recommend here is the Safety 1st Folding Booster seat ($15.99 to $26.99). This seat folds and fits easily into your car trunk or a closet. It's durable and you can't beat the price. We use this product constantly with our daughter and we see the product in use all over the place. Be prepared to carve your initials in the back if eating with a group of friends because there will be several identical seats around the table.

There is another type of booster known as a clip-on seat which secures on the end of a table. These cannot be used on a glass table or on a table with any kind of molding. Clip-ons should also never be used on a table that you really like because they can leave scratches and marks, even though the tips are rubber-coated.

Safety First

There is a Standard Consumer Safety Specification for Portable Hook-On Chairs called the ASTM F1235. This is another product category that the JPMA has a certification program for. The major requirements are:

❑ **A latching device to minimize accidental folding and no hazardous sharp edges, protrusions, or points before and after testing**
❑ **Protection from scissoring, coil springs, holes, and openings**
❑ **Chair drop test**
❑ **Static load test**
❑ **Push/pull test**
❑ **Disengagement and bounce test**
❑ **Labeling about not leaving child unattended, proper use and manufacturer information**
❑ **Instructional literature.**

There are specific warnings on the labels of these chairs, including:

❑ **Do not use on a glass or loose tabletop, single pedestal table, table leaf, or with table cloth or placemats.**
❑ **Check stability of table before seating child**
❑ **Do not place ordinary chair under this chair.**

There are specific safety instructions that must come with these chairs, including:

❑ **Child should be secured in the chair at all times by restraining system**

❏ **Do not use without all tips (or suction cups)
attached securely to table surface**
❏ **Keep seat and table surfaces clean**
❏ **Discontinue use when seated child can move chair
arms**
❏ **Do not allow other children or animals to play
near or walk under chair while in use.**

Your Budget

The most popular clip-on is the Graco Tot Lock ($29 to
$39). The Tot Lock is available with or without a tray,
has a padded seat and folds flat. If you're not too germ-
phobic, about your child eating directly off of a restaurant table that was probably cleaned with a bottle of
Windex and a dirty rag, you don't need the tray. Let's
face it—how clean are you really going to get the tray
after each use?

Mealtime Accessories

Bibs—You will see a vast array of baby bibs in anything
from fabric to hard molded plastic. Some have
appliqués; others have cute sayings, such as "Spit hap-
pens." The most important features in a fabric bib are
a Velcro closure (I would avoid bibs that go over the
head) and vinyl backing to prevent wet food from
penetrating baby's clothing. These fabric bibs get very
grungy very quickly. Some stains just won't come out.
A more practical approach may be to buy plastic or
vinyl bibs. They last a lot longer and are much
cheaper. For $2.99, you can buy Gerber's thin vinyl
bib that ties on like a smock. (Terry bibs range from
$3.99 to a ridiculous $8.99.) There is a special,
molded plastic bib called the Pelican ($3.49) that has
a large lip at the bottom to catch food. This is a popular item but the plastic tends to crack over time. No

matter what kind of bib you choose, the bigger, the better. A new rubberized bib by Bibco ($8.99) has unique snaps at the bottom that allow you to make the food-gathering lip at the bottom.

Suction bowl—A feeding bowl with a suction cup on the bottom to keep Junior from swatting it off the tray. This is a necessity and it costs about $3.99 (pretty comparable to the cost of a regular bowl, so you might as well go for the suction feature).

Hot water feeding dish—This is not such a necessity, but some parents like it. The hot water feeding dish ($6.99) is a hollow plastic suction bowl with an enclosed compartment for hot water that keeps the food warm. This is useful because it takes much longer than you can possibly imagine to feed a baby. Don't worry about the hot water burning the baby—there's a cap (like on a canteen) that twists on securely to prevent water spillage.

Rubber-coated feeding spoon—This is a kinder, gentler spoon for baby's delicate mouth. It is basically a necessity because the spoon is correctly sized for a baby's tiny mouth and the feeding process can get a little rough with an uncooperative baby. If you don't use a coated spoon, shoving it in and out can be irritating to Junior's mouth. The longer the handle, the better, because you have a shorter trip from the food bowl to the mouth. The spoon retails for approximately $1.49 to $2.49.

Splat Mat or Catch All—Why get aggravated? Invest in a vinyl tarp to cover the baby's feeding area. It will catch flying food and drops of grape juice before they land on the Scotchguard-protected light beige carpeting—a wise use of $7.99 for the Splat Mat by Children-on-the-Go or $9.99 for the Catch All by Prince Lionheart. If you're feeding the baby on easy-to-wipe linoleum, you could probably do without a tarp, or you could substitute an old plastic tablecloth.

Suction toy—If you need to distract baby while shoveling applesauce in his mouth, my favorite suction toy to stick on the food tray is Stand-up Man ($15). You just pull a string, and Stand-up Man does just that (it's more entertaining than it sounds). A suction-free toy will serve the same purpose, but you will have to bend down and pick it up seventeen times during one serving of strained carrots.

Kidco Food Mill—This is the most popular manual food grinder. It is portable, easy-to-use, and certainly beats cleaning out a Cuisinart on a daily basis ($11.99 to $13.99). For an extra $2 you can get a travel tote to go with it. First Years also makes a food grinder ($9.99) but it has not received good user feedback. It's supposedly very difficult to clean and the grinder doesn't produce smooth food. I would go with the KidCo.

Training Cup—This is an easy to use cup for the baby after he's off the nipple. These cups are covered and the child sips on a little spout. The Fisher-Price training cup has handles on both sides ($4.99) that regulate the flow of liquid as the child tips the cup to his mouth. In the beginning, kids pretty much just pour beverages directly down their shirts. Another popular training cup is the Playtex Spillproof cup ($4.99). This is the only cup that's advertised as leakproof when turned upside down. This cup always received an overwhelming response from my customers, and my own experience confirms it—these cups *do not* leak! The one that we had as kids seems to be out of vogue now, but if you're nostalgic or want to start a tradition you can still find the Tommy Tippy Cup ($4.99). It has a handle on either side, a round, weighted bottom, and different spout attachments so parents can regulate the liquid flow. There are many other cups as well—you'll experiment and find the one that works best for baby and you.

Duffel cool—This is a thermal pouch that comes with a hot/cold pack to keep bottles warm or cold ($11.99). Some diaper bags have a thermal compartment, but this item hangs from the stroller.

Baby Safe Feeder—This is an ingenious item designed by a dad who witnessed his son choking on a teething biscuit. When babies start to get teeth, they can inadvertently "bite off more than they can chew", posing a serious choking hazard. The baby safe feeder is a mesh bag that screws onto a plastic handle. Fruit, cookies, pretzels or any food that presents a choking hazard can be inserted into the mesh and baby can hold the handle and chew on the food without any danger of a big chunk coming off and lodging in his windpipe. For teething pain relief, frozen grapes, strawberries or bananas can be inserted. My daughter really enjoyed eating fruit this way and we enjoyed the peace of mind. The feeder retails for $8.99 and a pack of two replacement bags are $7.49.

Safety

MY FIRST PIECE of advice on safety is DON'T PANIC. I've known parents who spent the first weeks of their child's life sticking plugs into outlets and crawling around on their hands and knees baby proofing their home. Of course, the newborn was unable to move and was a lot more interested in sleeping than he was with their kitchen cabinets, but the parents had been whipped into such a frenzy that they lost, in my opinion, perspective. Until your child can crawl, you need not be deeply concerned with baby proofing. It's fine to do all of this sooner rather than later, but don't believe that any delay will endanger your child's life.

> ▶ **TIP:** A **choke hazard measure** ($1.99) is an important safety item. This is basically a cylinder that is the same size as a baby's windpipe. Any toy or part that fits in this cylinder is a choking hazard. If you want to save the $1.99, a toilet paper roll provides the same measure. You should also have a bottle of Ipecac on hand, a substance that induces vomiting in the unlikely event that your baby ingests poison.

I've said it earlier in this book, and I'll say it again— the most important safety precaution is NEVER LEAVE YOUR CHILD UNATTENDED. Keeping an eye on little Aldo at all times will prevent the majority of possible accidents. Remember: no product can substitute for your attention. You should still pull your child away from the outlet and say "no"; safety products are simply the last line of defense. That leaves two other scenarios to make provisions for: when Aldo does something in those two seconds when you turn away to see if the pasta is done, and when Aldo does something right before your own very horrified eyes. Safety products will help you minimize the danger of these moments and maybe give you some peace of mind as Hurricane (Your Child's Name Here) blows through your home.

You'll notice that I've given prices, but I'm skipping the Your Budget section. Nothing in this category costs very much, and, at risk of sounding like an insurance commercial, I can't imagine wanting to pinch pennies when it comes to your baby's safety.

Outlet Plugs

- Must Have
- 6 months to school age
- Ridiculous to borrow
- Price range: $1.99 to $3.99

THE MOST THREATENING household risks to a crawling baby are electrical outlets because they are at eye level and are compelling holes into which curious fingers can be inserted. Unless you're Fred and Wilma Flintstone, you've got outlets all over your house. Luckily, there are about as many ways to make outlets safe as there are rea-

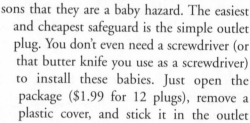

sons that they are a baby hazard. The easiest and cheapest safeguard is the simple outlet plug. You don't even need a screwdriver (or that butter knife you use as a screwdriver) to install these babies. Just open the package ($1.99 for 12 plugs), remove a plastic cover, and stick it in the outlet where you would ordinarily stick an electrical plug. The bad news is that now you can't use the outlet and sooner than you think Junior will figure out how to remove that plug.

A more secure alternative (get that butter knife) is an outlet box that goes over the switch plate ($2.99). This allows the outlet to remain usable while out of the baby's reach. Before purchasing these, examine your switch-plates to determine whether they are fastened by a center screw or a top and bottom screw (still not brain surgery).

The most aesthetically pleasing outlet cover is the Safe-Plate by Selfix ($3.99). This replaces your existing switchplate (get that butter knife) with a plate that features spring-loaded outlet covers. When a plug is removed from the outlet, the cover automatically blocks the opening. All of these products are interchangeable. You might have fifty electrical outlets in your house, but your baby might only be interested in one. You will probably use several different types of outlet covers, depending on your needs.

Corner Guards

- Might Want
- 6 months to preschool
- Bad to borrow
- Price range $1.99 to $59.99

SHARP EDGES ON furniture present a possible hazard to crawling and walking babies. There are a couple of kinds of corner guards made specifically to soften these sharp edges. The first are little plastic ends that you affix to corners with double-sided tape (Safety 1st makes a package of four for $1.99). Unfortunately, they don't stay on too well. I know a ten-month-old who showed no interest in the living room's coffee table until his parents safeguarded the corners. He is now a regular visitor to the sharp edges of the coffee table, where he likes to take off the corner guards and hand them to his dad. A better device, the bumper guard, which is sort of a padded "garter", goes around the entire edge of the table. It's not attractive, but it provides the best protection against head-bonking. Ofna makes the bumper guard in four sizes, from $39.99 to $59.99.

Safety Gates

- Might Want
- 6 months to preschool
- OK to borrow
- Price range: $16.99 to $69.99

A GATE PREVENTS the baby from going into areas where you don't want him. Many types of safety gates are available; your decision will largely be based on where you are using it and how wide an opening you are trying to block. Obviously, a staircase would be gated off, as would any area with hazardous items (or just items that you remotely like). You might also consider gating off the kitchen, so

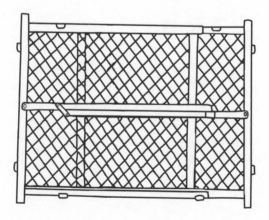

you don't have to lock the drawers and cabinets. Before you go to buy a gate, be sure to measure your doorway because gates come in all shapes and sizes. I list safety gates as Might Want, but that depends on your lifestyle and on how many floors you have. If you have more than one floor, these are a Must Have.

Safety First

The ASTM F1004 Standard Consumer Safety Specification for Gates includes general requirements, such as:

❏ **Finish of parts and type of fasteners**
❏ **Size of openings, height, strength of top rails and framing components, bottom spacing, and configuration of uppermost edge**
❏ **A permanent and conspicuous label advising user to install according to manufacturer's instructions, warning that this product will not prevent all accidents and to never leave the child unattended.**
❏ **When using a gate at the top of stairs, you must use a hardware-mounted gate which is screwed into the wall.**

> ▶ **SAFETY TIP:** Accordion gates with crosshatch pattern must have a solid tape across the top to prevent the sharp edges from harming the baby. Most new accordion gates have this, but if you borrow one, keep this in mind. If you need to watch your child while using the gate, it defeats the purpose. Also, accordion gates should never be used at the top of the stairs because they create a natural ladder for the baby to climb on.

Parenting requires many sacrifices, including ruining your walls. The simplest hardware-mounted gate is the Evenflo 1048 ($18.99). There is one exception—a pressure-mounted gate, the Kidco Gateaway ($85, available in black, white and silver), is secure enough for the top of the stairs. This gate features four individually adjustable pressure points that will secure tightly to uneven walls and moldings. This gate also features a door with a release on top (simple for adults to operate but not babies and toddlers) so that adults can walk through easily.

Generally, pressure-mounted gates are better for keeping the baby out of rooms like the kitchen. You don't have to go through the hassle of screwing them into walls, and if for some reason they do get pushed down, the baby will not fall down a flight of stairs, just into the room that you are trying to keep him out of. A good thing about keeping the baby out of the kitchen is that there is less necessity to baby proof the oven and cabinets. The simplest pressure-mounted gate is the Evenflo 662 ($29.99), though it can be hard to use on an uneven doorway.

A nice product is the Extra-WideSoft Gate by Evenflo. This is a washable nylon-and-mesh gate that folds into a carrying case. It's also good for uneven doorways in your house or Grandma's. This is a good thing to have if you are going away for the weekend or renting a vacation house. This retails for $34.99.

Drawer, Cabinet, and Toilet Locks

- Must Have
- 6 months to preschool
- Bad to Borrow
- Price Range: $1.99 to $9.99

ONCE JUNIOR IS really on the go and starts becoming fascinated with sharp knives and Drano, you need to start locking drawers, cabinets, and even the toilet—you'll never know when he's in the mood for a swim or a refreshing sip of water. Selfix makes Safe-Lok (three for $3.99/six for $5.99) for cabinets and drawers, which lets them open just one inch while preventing them from slamming shut on the baby's fingers. However, Safe-Lok is somewhat of a pain to install because it requires that two pieces be screwed on—one on the stationary cabinetry and one on the moving drawer or cabinet door. Gerber makes a spring-action drawer latch (four for $4.99) that is easier to install on drawers than the Selfix because there is only one L-shaped piece of plastic to deal with. Like the Selfix, the Gerber model also prevents finger-slamming mishaps. Regardless of the type you choose, these locks are easy for adults to get around but impossible for toddlers to figure out, so don't worry—they're not nearly as annoying as the child-proof caps on drugs.

To avoid installing any kind of hardware at all, a very simple way to lock cabinets with knobs on them is with a Cabinet Lock ($1.99). This is a small horseshoe-shaped piece of plastic with a bar that opens with pressure. In a pinch, thick rubber bands will also do the job. Rubber bands can even be better because they can stretch to virtually any size.

To secure the commode, you can choose Selfix's Lid-Lok ($9.99) or the Toilet Lock from Safety 1st ($5.99). The Lid-Lock is a clip that secures the lid to the seat, which still enables an adult to open the toilet lid with the seat attached (good for daddies and a pain for mommies) but makes it too heavy for a toddler to lift up. The Toilet Lock completely closes off the toilet with two buckles on the sides connected to a belt that goes across the top of the toilet lid. The belt locks on the top like a seat belt that is easy for adults but impossible for toddlers to operate.

Door and Stove Knob Covers

- Might Want
- 9 months to preschool
- Bad to Borrow
- Price Range: $1.99 to $5.99

A KNOB COVER is a plastic ring that goes over the door knob so that a toddler cannot turn it and enter a room. You can get a pack of three for $1.99.

Safety 1st once made covers for stove knobs, but they were recalled because they were found to be flammable. To baby proof the kitchen, there's the Shield-a-Burn ($19.99), which is a heat-resistant plastic plate that adheres to the top of the stove, blocking the burners. The problem is that the stove's heat tends to affect the adhesive and the Shield-a-Burn falls off. Also, if the baby is tall enough to reach the flame, he is tall enough to pull down the Shield-a-Burn. I wouldn't bother with this product—it's safer just to keep the baby away from the stove.

VCR Lock

- Might Want
- 9 months to graduate school
- Bad to borrow
- Price: $4.99

FOR YOU ELECTRONICS aficionados, there is a VCR lock ($4.99) that keeps the baby from shoving mashed potatoes into the VCR. This rectangular plastic piece blocks the opening where you insert tapes.

Cord Holders and Shorteners

- Must Have
- Birth to school age
- Bad to borrow
- Price range: $1.99 to $2.99

THERE ARE CORD HOLDERS ($1.99) that lift speaker wire off the floor and cord shorteners ($2.99) that wind up excess cord and speaker wire. There are also cord shorteners for window blind cord, which can present a strangling hazard. These wind the cord inside an enclosed spool so there is no slack. You can also use a hook attached to the wall to wind the excess blind cord around or a clothespin to wind up cord and pin it up and out of baby's reach.

Appendices

When Will You Need It?

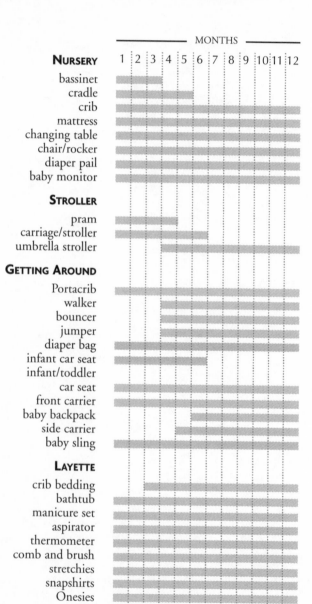

	MONTHS											
NURSERY	1	2	3	4	5	6	7	8	9	10	11	12
bassinet												
cradle												
crib												
mattress												
changing table												
chair/rocker												
diaper pail												
baby monitor												
STROLLER												
pram												
carriage/stroller												
umbrella stroller												
GETTING AROUND												
Portacrib												
walker												
bouncer												
jumper												
diaper bag												
infant car seat												
infant/toddler car seat												
front carrier												
baby backpack												
side carrier												
baby sling												
LAYETTE												
crib bedding												
bathtub												
manicure set												
aspirator												
thermometer												
comb and brush												
stretchies												
snapshirts												
Onesies												

MONTHS

	1	2	3	4	5	6	7	8	9	10	11	12
infant gowns	■	■	■									
blanket sleeper						■	■	■	■	■	■	■
hats	■	■	■									
booties	■	■	■	■	■	■	■	■	■	■	■	■
receiving blanket	■	■	■	■	■	■	■	■	■	■	■	■
wool blanket	■	■	■	■	■	■	■	■	■	■	■	■
hooded towels	■	■	■	■	■	■	■	■	■	■	■	■
washcloths	■	■	■	■	■	■	■	■	■	■	■	■

FOOD

	1	2	3	4	5	6	7	8	9	10	11	12
high chair				■	■	■	■	■	■	■	■	■
bottles/nipples	■	■	■	■	■	■	■	■	■	■	■	■
pacifiers	■	■	■	■	■	■	■	■	■	■	■	■
breast pump	■	■	■	■	■	■	■	■	■	■	■	■
nursing pads	■	■	■	■	■	■	■	■	■	■	■	■
bibs	■	■	■	■	■	■	■	■	■	■	■	■

SAFETY

	1	2	3	4	5	6	7	8	9	10	11	12
outlet plugs				■	■	■	■	■	■	■	■	■
toilet locks				■	■	■	■	■	■	■	■	■
doorknob covers				■	■	■	■	■	■	■	■	■
gates				■	■	■	■	■	■	■	■	■
bath seat				■	■	■	■	■	■	■	■	■
cord shortener				■	■	■	■	■	■	■	■	■
cord holder				■	■	■	■	■	■	■	■	■
table guards				■	■	■	■	■	■	■	■	■
cabinet locks				■	■	■	■	■	■	■	■	■
drawer locks				■	■	■	■	■	■	■	■	■
stove knob covers				■	■	■	■	■	■	■	■	■

Different Products for Different Budgets

	Lotto Winner	*Lots of Money*	*Lots of Love*
NURSERY			
Crib	Wrought Iron. **$1,000**	Bonavita Pamela. $530	Simmons Matino. $249
Mattress	Allergy-free Innerspring. **$149**	Simmons Maxipedic Innerspring. **$119**	Comfort Foam mattress. **$99**
Changing Table	Morgeau three-drawer changer with flip kit. **$700**	Three-drawer dresser ($299) with contoured pad ($30). **$329**	Badger Deluxe Foldaway open changer. **$99**
Rocking Chair	Leather glider with matching ottoman. **$700**	Shermag glider and ottoman. $350	Basic rocking chair. **$129**
Diaper Pail	Hand-painted and decorated. **$50.**	Diaper Genie. **$30.**	Pack of deodorizers. **$2.**
Hamper	Hand-painted and decorated. **$50.**	Wicker. **$25.**	Laundry bag. **$6.**
Monitor	In-wall room-to-room system. **$1,000**	Fisher-Price monitor. **$60**	"Did you hear the baby?" **Free**
STROLLER			
Carriage	Silver Stream by Silver Cross. **$1,500**	Perego Milano carriage/stroller. $349	Graco LiteRider stroller. **$79**

	Lotto Winner	Lots of Money	Lots of Love
Stroller	Perego Milano carriage. **$289**	Perego Pliko. **$229**	Maclaren Day Tripper. **$149**
Rain Shield	Two covers. **$50.**	One cover. **$20.**	Umbrella. **$5**

GETTING AROUND

	Lotto Winner	Lots of Money	Lots of Love
Portacrib	5-way Pack 'N Play. **$129**	Bassinett Pack 'N Play. **$90**	Graco Pack 'N Play. **$70**
Infant Car Seat	Century Vante. **$100**	Graco SnugRide **$79.**	Century 1000, birth to 40 lbs. **$49**
Car Seat	Brittax Roundabout. **$200**	Century Bravo. **$99**	Century 1000, birth to 40 lbs. **$49**
Infant Seat	Chicco Rocker. **$99**	Fisher-Price Infant/Toddler Rocker. **$39**	Not necessary.
Diaper Bag	Kate Spade. **$300**	Baby Mania fake Fendi. **$100**	Portable changing pad. **$7**
Front Carrier	Nanny. **$500 per week.**	Baby Bjorn. **$79**	Snugli. **$29**

LAYETTE

	Lotto Winner	Lots of Money	Lots of Love
Bumper Set (quilt, bumper, dust ruffle, sheet)	Bebe Chic complete set. **$800**	Littlelinens.com blue oxford stripe matching bumper set. **$295**	Solid color bumper. **$40**
Terry Covers	4 zipper covers. **$24 each**	2 elastic covers. **$19 each**	Towels from the closet
Waterproof Sheets	2 sheets. **$10 each.**	2 combination sheets and quilted pads. **$15 each.**	Washcloth.

	Lotto Winner	Lots of Money	Lots of Love
Quilted Pads	2 pads. $15 each	Included above.	1 pad. **$12.**
Crib Bib	2 sets. **$16 each.**	1 set. **$16.**	Cloth diapers. **$21/dozen.**
Crib Sheets	4 sheets to match the bumper set. **$30 each.**	2 sheets to match the bumper, at **$25 each**, plus 2 Carter's,at **$9 each.**	4 Carter's sheets. **$9 each.**
Bathtub	Large tub with stand. **$45**	Evenflo Infant/Toddler tub. **$19**	Sponge in the sink. **$7**
Nail Care Set	Tiffany set. **$50**	Separate scissors and clippers. **$10**	Clippers. **$2**
Aspirator	**$3**	**$3**	**$3**
Thermometer	Thermoscan. $59	Digital $10	Rectal $4
Stretchies	6 Mini Basic cotton imports. **$20 each**.	4 Carter's terry. **$10 each.**	2 Carter's terry, at **$10 each**, and 2 Onesies. **$5 each.**
Comb and Brush	Tiffany silver set. **$100**	Designer. **$20.**	Basic. **$4**
Booties	Embroidered. **$25.**	Padders. **$8**	Socks. **$2**
Hat	Barney's Cashmere. **$30.**	Cotton Stretchie. **$8**	The one you got at the hospital.
Receiving Blankets	6 Mini Basic. **$20 each.**	3 Mini Basic, at **$20 each**, and 3 Carter's, at **$7 each.**	3 Carter's. **$7 each.**
Hooded Towels	6 Rockaby. **$20 each.**	2 Rockaby, at **$20 each,** and 2 Carter's, at **$7 each.**	2 Carter's. **$7 each.**

	Lotto Winner	*Lots of Money*	*Lots of Love*
Washcloths	6 Rockaby. **$8 each**	4 2-packs. **$4 each**	Use your own

FOOD

	Lotto Winner	*Lots of Money*	*Lots of Love*
Pacifiers	3 packs of Utti Mam decorative. **$5 each**	1 pack of Utti Mam at **$5** each and 2 Gerber Nuk at **$2 each**	2 Gerber Nuk. **$2 each**
Bottles	12 Ansa decorated. **$4 each**	6 Ansa decorated, at **$4 each**, and 6 generic, at **$1.29 each**.	6 generic. **$1.29 each.**
High Chair	Antique wooden. **$500**	Perego Prima Pappa, adjustable on wheels. **$169**	Safety 1st Folding Booster. **$17**
Breast Pump	Medela Lactina, purchased. **$500.**	Medela Lactina, rented. **$1 per day**	Gerber manual. **$20**
Bibs	12 embroidered. **$9 each**	6 cloth. $6 each	Cloth diapers and napkins
TOTAL	**$9,275**	**$3,595.74**	**$1,174**

Manufacturers and Catalogs:

Aprica U.S.A.
310-639-6387 www.apricausa.com

Avent America
800-54-AVENT www.aventamerica.com

Baby Bjorn
800-593-5522 www.babybjorn.com

Baby Jogger Co.
509-457-0925 www.babyjogger.com

Baby Trend
800-328-7368 www.babytrend.com

Badger Basket
800-873-0261 www.badgerbasket.com

Basic Comfort (wipe warmer)
800-456-8687 www.basiccomfort.com

C&T Furniture (Sorelle)
201-461-9444 www.sorellefurniture.com

Camp Kazoo (Boppy)
888-77-BOPPY www.campkazoo.com

Century Products/Graco
800-345-4109 www.gracobaby.com

Child Craft
812-883-3111 www.childcraftind.com

Combi International
800-992-6624 www.combi-intl.com

Cosco (Dorel Juvenile Group)
    800-544-1108   www.djgusa.com

Dutailier
    800-363-9817   www.dutailier.com

Evenflo
    800-233-5921   www.evenflo.com

The First Years
    800-225-0382   www.thefirstyears.com

Fisher-Price, Inc.
    800-432-5437   www.fisher-price.com

Gerber Products Company
    800-4-GERBER   www.gerber.com

Gerry Baby Products (see Evenflo)
    800-233-5921   www.evenflo.com

Graco Children's Products
    800-345-4109   www.gracobaby.com

Hanna Anderson
    800-222-0544   www.hannaanderson.com

Inglesina Baby
    877-486-5112   www.inglesina.com

Kelty
    800-423-2320   www.kelty.com

Kidco
    800-553-5529   www.kidcoinc.com

Kolcraft Enterprises, Inc.
    800-453-7673   www.kolcraft.com

Lands' End Kids
    800-356-4444   www.landsend.com

Lillian Vernon Kids
   800-285-5555   www.lillianvernon.com

Little Tykes Company
   800-321-0183   www.littletykes.com

L.L Bean Kids
   800-341-4341   www.llbean.com

Maclaren Strollers
   877-442-4622   www.maclarenbaby.com

Medela, Inc.
   800-435-8316   www.medela.com

Morigeau Furniture USA
   800-326-2121   www.morigeau.com

Noel Joanna, Inc. (NoJo)
   800-854-8760   www.nojo.com

One Step Ahead
   800-274-8440   www.onestepahead.com

Peg Perego USA, Inc.
   800-671-1701   www.perego.com

Playskool (Hasbro)
   800-752-9755   www.playskool.com

Playtex Products, Inc
   800-222-0453   www.playtexbaby.com

Prince Lionheart
   800-544-1132   www.princelionheart.com

Ragazzi Furniture
   888-324-7886   www.ragazzi.com

Right Start
   800-548-8531   www.rightstart.com

Rochelle Furniture
   717-834-3031   www.rochellefurniture.com

Safety 1st, Inc.
   800-723-3065   www.safety1st.com

Safety Zone
   800-999-3030   www.safetyzone.com

Sassy, Inc.
   800-323-6336   www.sassybaby.com

Simmons Juvenile Products
   920-982-2140   www.simmonsjp.com

Simo USA Inc.
   800-SIMO4ME   www.simo.ca

Summer Infant Products
   800-9BOUNCR   www.summerinfant.com

Thermoscan (Braun)
   800-327-7226   www.braun.com

Today's Kids
   800-258-8697   www.todayskids.com

Tough Traveler Ltd.
   800-GO-TOUGH   www.toughtraveler.com

Organizations:

CPSC
   800-638-CPSC   www.cpsc.gov

JPMA
   856-638-0420   www.jpma.org

NHTSA
   888-DASH-2-DOT   www.nhtsa.gov

Index

activity gym, 22
airplane travel, 107, 115, 123
Albee's, 13, 79
Amazon.com, 21
assembly, 11, 16, 20

Babies "R" Us, 20
baby carriers. *See* backpacks;
    front carriers; sling carriers
Baby Gap, 66, 72
baby monitors, 18, 22,
    63–65, 65, 196
baby proofing, 185. *See also*
    safety products
babysitter. See caregiver
backpacks, 16, 29,
    133–137, 196
Back to Basics, 21
bassinets, 30, 47–50, 96,
    98, 152, 196
bathing accessories, 90–92
bath seats, 18, 89–90, 197
bathtub, 18, 31, 85–88, 196
bedding, 74–80, 196
beds, 42–43
bibs, 127, 130, 131,
    181–182, 197
blanket, receiving, 72–73,
    197

blanket sleeper, 70–71, 197
booster seats, 178–181
booties, 72
borrowing. *See specific
    products*
bottle and nipple brush, 172
bottle rack, for dishwasher,
    172
bottles and nipples, 16–17,
    18, 31, 168–173, 197
bottle warmer, 172
bouncer seats, 18, 22, 30,
    138–140, 196
bowl, suction, 182
breast–feeding equipment,
    16, 159–168
breast milk, storage, 167
breast pumps, 16, 163–167,
    197
breast shields, 168
budget, product review by,
    198–201
bumper, 76–78, 79

cabinet locks, 190–191,
    197
canopies, 102, 104, 109, 153
car accessories, 127
caregiver, 13, 31–33, 64

carriages, 95–103. *See also* strollers
  borrowing, 28, 29, 97
  pram, 93, 95–98, 108, 196
  safety issues, 25, 100
  selection factors, 93–95
  twin, 108–111
carriage/strollers, 98–103, 108, 196
carriers. *See* backpacks; front carriers; sling carriers
car seat cover, 20
car seats
  accessories, 120
  for airplane travel, 123
  base for, 123–124
  bib for, 127
  borrowing, 29, 30, 116, 120, 122
  headrests for, 122–123, 127
  infant, 120, 121–125, 196
  infant/toddler, 117–120, 196
  installation, 26
  loaner, 14
  product review by budget, 199
  safety issues, 26, 115, 116
  selection factors, 114–117
  shopping time line, 196
  with stroller travel systems, 99, 125–127

car seat strap pad, 120
catalog shopping, 12, 17, 20–22, 202–205
chain stores, 9–10, 16, 17–18, 64
chairs. *See* high chairs; portable hook–on chair; rockers
changing pad, 53, 56–57, 155, 157
changing tables, 30, 52–57, 152, 196
clip–on seat, 25, 179–180
clothing, 22, 30–31, 66–69, 72, 196
college expenses, 33–34
comb/brush, 84, 196
comforter, 79–80
common sense, importance of, 27, 37
comparative shopping, 12
Consumer Products Safety Commission (CPSC), 23–25, 27, 89, 205
cord holders and shorteners, 193, 197
corner guards, 187–188, 197
cradles, 51–52, 196
credit card shopping, 11, 13, 20–22, 33
crib bib, 78

cribs, 38–45
  borrowing, 30, 38, 41–42
  drop sides, 40, 41, 44
  not to buy from a catalog,
    17
  portable, 14, 149–154, 196
  safety issues, 25, 39–40
  shopping time line, 196
  that convert to beds, 42–43
crib sheets, 76, 79
crib wedges, 46–47, 48
cup, training, 183–184
cushions, wedge–shaped,
  46–47, 48

delivery, 11, 13, 18, 20
deposit, 11, 20
diaper bags, 21, 154–158,
  196
diaper pails, 18, 57–60, 196
diapers, 57–58, 71, 157
diaper service, 58
door knob covers, 192, 197
drawer locks, 190–191, 197
dust ruffle, 78, 79

education expenses, 33–34
electrical outlet plugs,
  186–187, 197
E–Toys, 21

feeding. *See also* booster
seats; bottles and nipples;
breast–feeding; high chairs
  accessories, 181–184
  high chair tray, 175, 176,
    177
  product review by budget,
    201
  shopping time frame, 197
  utensils, 32, 182
  walker tray, 145
feeding dish, hot water, 182
feeding mats, 182
financial planning, 33–34
first aid book, 85
food mill, 183
front carriers, 16, 22, 29,
  109, 128–132, 196
furniture
  assembly, 11
  borrowing, 30
  from independent stores,
    15–16
  nursery. *See* changing
    tables; cradles; cribs;
    rockers
  that "grows up" with your
    child, 38, 54

garage sales, 22
gates, safety, 25, 188–190,
  197
gifts, 13, 19, 22, 138

glider rocker, 16, 61
gown, 69, 197

hamper, 60
Hannah Anderson, 21
hat, 71–72, 197
high chairs, 25, 30, 32,
   173–177, 197
hood/canopy, 102, 104, 109
hook–on seat, 25, 179–180
hot/cold pack, 184

Ikea, 38
independent stores, 9–10,
   15–17
infant carrier, from infant
   car seat, 121
infant seats. *See* bath seats;
   bouncer seats; car seats
infant sleeping bag, 69
interior decorating, 43–44,
   51, 61–62, 80

jogging stroller, 106–108
jumpers, 147–149, 196
Juvenile Products
   Manufacturers Association
   (JPMA), 25, 100, 174,
   180, 205

knob covers, 192, 197

L. L. Bean Kids, 21

Lands' End Kids, 21
lap pad, 57
laundry bag, 56
laundry tip, 69
layette. *See also* bathing
   accessories; bedding;
   clothing
   personal choice in the,
      66–67
   product review by budget,
      199–201
   shopping time frame, 196
   store selection, 12, 18
Lillian Vernon Kids, 21
loaner items, 14, 18, 94,
   105
locks, 58, 190–191, 192,
   197

manicure set, 82, 196
manufacturers
   contact information,
      202–205
   liability of, 24
   reporting malfunctions to,
      43
   as a resource, 4, 15, 30,
      120, 140, 176
mat, feeding, 182
mattresses. *See also* pads
   bassinet, 47, 48, 49, 50
   carriage/pram, 97
   cradle, 51

crib, 31, 38, 40, 45–47

portable playpen, 151, 152

shopping time line, 196

mirrors, 22, 127

monitors. *See* baby monitors

Moses basket, 49, 50, 97,
98, 132

mosquito netting, 111, 151,
154

nanny. *See* caregiver

nasal aspirator, 84, 196

National Highway Traffic
Safety Administration
(NHTSA), 25–26, 115,
125, 205

nursery

product review by budget,
198

shopping time frame,
196

shopping tips, 37–38

nursing pads, 167, 197

nursing pillows, 18,
160–161

nursing stools, 161–163

Onesies, 68–69, 196

One Step Ahead, 22

online shopping, 20–22,
202–205

ottomans, 62

outlet plugs, 186–187, 197

out-of-season shopping, 21

pacifier case, 81

pacifier clip, 81

pacifiers, 18, 31, 80, 197

packaging

keep the, 18, 63–64, 91,
131, 148

re–boxing by the store, 18

pads

changing, 53, 56–57, 155,
157

lap, 57

nursing, 167

quilted, 75

pajamas, 70–71

part replacement, 16, 30, 43

Perfectly Safe, 21

playpens, portable, 17,
150–154, 196

playsuits, 69, 70

play yards, 25

poisoning, 185

portable cribs, 14,
149–154, 196

portable hook-on chair, 25,
179–180

portable playpens, 17,
150–154, 196

"portacribs," 150

prams, 93, 95–98, 108, 196

price
chain store, 17, 18
expense vs. quality, 14
hidden charges, 20
product review by,
198–201
ranges in book, 4, 5

quilted pad, 75

recalls, 26–27, 115, 120,
125, 143, 192
receiving blanket, 72–73,
197
rentals, 16, 165–166. *See
also* loaner items
repairs, 9, 12, 15, 16, 95,
97, 105
returns, 9, 11, 18, 21,
63–64, 131, 148
Right Start, 20, 21–22
rockers, 16, 17, 30, 60–63,
196

safety gates, 188–190, 197
safety issues. *See also* recalls
bassinets, 49
bath seats, 89–90
bath sponge, 86
bathtub spout, 91
booster seats, 180–181
bouncer seats, 138

carriages and strollers, 25,
100, 110
car seats, 26, 115, 116
changing tables, 54
choking, 185
cradles, 51, 52
cribs, 39–40
flame-retardant material,
69
high chairs, 174–175
mattresses, 45–46
never leave your child
unattended, 23, 27, 54,
90, 185
pacifier clip, 81
product safety regulation,
23–27
safety gates, 25, 189
seat belts during preg-
nancy, 126
walkers, 25, 145–146
safety products, 18, 21, 31,
185–193, 197
Safety Zone, 21
sales, 18, 22, 64
seat belts during pregnancy,
126
seats. See bath seats; booster
seats; bouncer seats; car
seats; clip–on seat
shades, 127, 151
sheets, 74–75, 76, 79, 151

shopping. *See also* manufacturers
  bargaining power, 17, 18, 49–50
  comparative, 12
  five commandments of, 18
  known brand names, 11
  out-of-season, 21
  product review by budget, 198–201
  relationship with staff, 6, 9–10, 12–13, 15
  for sales, 18, 22, 64
  store hours, 11
  store location, 14
  time frame for, 5, 19, 22–23, 28–29, 196–197
  where to go, 9–11
sling carriers, 132–133, 196
snapshirt, 67–68, 196
sponges, bathing, 86, 91–92
sprayer nozzle, 91
stain remover, 75
sterilizers, 172–173
stove knob covers, 192, 197
stretchy, 70, 196
strollers. *See also* carriages
  accessories, 111–112
  airplane travel, 107
  with attachable car seat, 99
  borrowing, 29, 102, 109
  caregiver's input, 32

carriage/strollers, 98–103
  from catalogs/online, 17, 20
  from chain stores, 15, 18
  "disposable," 94
  from independent stores, 15
  jogging, 106–108
  product review by budget, 198–199
  repairs, 15, 18
  safety issues, 25, 100, 110
  selection factors, 15, 93–95
  shopping time frame, 196
  and traveling, 107, 125–127
  twin, 108–111
  umbrella, 32, 93, 100, 102, 103–106, 109, 112, 157, 196
superstores, 19–20. *See also* chain stores
swings, 17, 30, 33, 138, 141–144

tax issues, 529 Plan, 34
teething, 184
terry cover, 56
thermal pouch, 184
thermometers, 82–83, 91, 196

time frame for shopping, 5, 19, 22–23, 28–29, 196–197
tippy cup, 183
toilet locks, 190–191, 197
towels, hooded, 73, 197
toys
    bath, 91–92
    black-and-white, 22
    from catalogs, 21
    newborn, not to borrow, 31
    for stroller, 111–112
    suction, 183
    for walker, 146
    wooden, 21

Toys "R" Us, 17, 18
twins, 108–111

umbrella strollers. See strollers, umbrella

VCR lock, 192
video monitors, 65
visor, rubber, 91

walkers, 18, 25, 33, 144–147, 196
washcloths, 74, 197
web sites, 20–22, 202–205
when will you need it, 5, 19, 22–23, 28–29, 196–197